DAD

Becoming the Father Every Child Needs and Every Wife Desires

SCOT ANDERSON

Winword
publishing house

Phoenix, Arizona

DAD

FIRST EDITION

Published by **Winword Publishing House**
3520 E. Brown Road
Mesa, AZ 85213
480-985-6156

ISBN 13 1-978-1-58588-025-6

DAD, Becoming the Father Every Child Needs and Every Wife Desires

Printed in Canada

To order or for more information, contact us at:

480-985-6156

or visit: www.DadMomBook.com

DAD

TABLE OF CONTENTS

DAD

DAD

I dedicate this book, first, to my Father God. Thank you for always being there and for giving me nothing but the best in my life.

I also dedicate this book to my best friend and the love of my life. Although you are just the neighbor lady who doesn't really know me… (That was kind of funny!) Seriously, Holly, without you as my wife, a part of me would be missing. You have helped me become a better person. You are the greatest gift God has ever given me. Thank you for backing me up, pushing me toward excellence, and, all the while, making life an amazing experience. I love you so much and look forward to growing old together with you. You are truly a blessing from God who adds so much laughter to my life. I watch you with our children and see how natural being a great mom is to you, and the children and I just have to say, "Thank God for Mom."

I would also like to dedicate this book to my amazing four boys: Laken, Heath, Baylor, and Peyton. You four are the best kids in the world. I am so proud of each and every one of you. You add so much joy and happiness to my life. I'm so thankful for the great memories we've created together so far, and I'm even more excited about all the great times we'll have over the next eighty years of my life. I love each of you so much.

I would also like to dedicate this book to my parents—the two best parents in the world. Although we didn't have much money growing up, really, we had it all. We had great memories and great times. You created a home full of love, acceptance, security, and happiness. Thank you for laying down your lives for us.

Dad, I have said this many times: I write this book based on what you did as a father. You changed generations to come because you had a father's heart. And today, you and I are best friends who love to be around each other—to go fishing and skiing every year together, to golf each week together, and to just talk. I'm the luckiest "kid" in the world because I have the greatest father.

Mom, you, too, are the best! I want to write a book on a mother's heart, and it will be all about you. You were the best mom, always putting your needs after ours. We, too, are best friends today. I love our weekly lunches and daily phone calls. I'm the luckiest "kid" in the world because I have the greatest mother.

To my brother and my best friend (I have a lot of best friends!), the person who I've probably spent more time with than anyone else on the planet. We could have fun with two spoons and a matchbox car out in the 110-degree heat (Mom said it was good for us). I love all our memories of growing up together—playing car soccer, car football, car basketball, car wars, throw the cat in the pool, car hockey, car Olympics, car racing, car polo, car horseshoes, car star wars, kick the cat, car wrestling, car dodgeball, car foosball, see how many flips the cat can do down the stairs, car bowling, car… (all we had were matchbox cars and marbles). You're a great father, husband, and friend, and you inspire me to be the best I can be.

I would also like to thank Dave, my best friend since the third grade. You made this book successful with all your hard work, wisdom beyond your years, and dedication. I thank God for all the great memories we had growing up fighting over the same girls. (Though we never got one of those girls—cruising in that thirty-foot-long, four-door Buick, wondering why no girls would get into the car!) Thank you for making church, camps, and life so much fun.

I also would like to thank Derek another one of my best friends. Thank you for the tremdous amount of work you did on the cover of this book. I love everything except the flaps. You're a great friend, who always makes me laugh. Never forget the poppyseeds, or the day

I perfected my cartwheel. Jesus is Lord! Also I am still your comanding officer and will always be.

I would also like to thank John. Another best friend. You would be impossible to replace. I have never had a friend who gives like you do. We have a great time together, even when you whoop me at DOA. Few moments in my life measure to when you caught that monster fish in Cape Cod . Thanks for all you do, all you give, and thanks for the success you brought into my life.

Finally, I would like to thank my tenth grade English teacher and wrestling coach whom I have not seen in twenty years. But if somehow you read this, know you are a big reason for my being who I am today. Though your techniques might be criticized today—hitting me on the head with that large pencil whenever I didn't get my homework done, erasing the board with me when I didn't get my homework done, thumping me on the ear when I didn't get my homework done—they were always done in fun, with humor, and it was what I needed to get motivated. Your teaching style forced me to learn to write and to write with excellence. Without you, I probably wouldn't have graduated from college, nor written a book. Thank you, Mr. Lee!

When reading this book, please understand that we all make mistakes—especially we fathers. We all have made mistakes and will probably make a lot more in the future. Being a great father isn't about making no mistakes. Being a great father is about learning not to make the same mistake over and over again. Being a great father isn't about our lack of character in a few bad situations. It is our overall character that we demonstrate to our kids throughout each day and throughout our lives.

My father, after whom I pattern my life, may have messed up a bunch when I was a child. If he did, though, I don't remember it because all the good outweighed the bad. I can't remember the bad because there was too much good in our lives.

Also, realize that great fathers are not born; they are developed. Every father has inside him the potential to be a great dad. But like anything in life, it takes understanding how to be great, then choosing to be great, and, finally, a lot of practice to be great. Being a great dad isn't something you just try or even do for eighteen years. It has to be something you do for the rest of your life because your being great comes from the inside—from the heart. You have to dedicate yourself to never stop growing and to never stop changing and to always pursuing being the best dad you can be.

I write this book, not from my experience of being a great father, but from my experience of being a son of a great father. That's a different twist. You see, I can't write this book on the premise that I have "arrived." I can't say, "Look at me. I've done it. I was a great dad. I raised my nine-year-old to perfection. He doesn't do drugs, hardly ever cusses, and we just got him off cigarettes (that is a joke)."

I can't say, "Look at what I have done." But I can say look at what my father has done. And I can share with you what I experienced as a son—how my dad made me feel and what was developed in me because of my relationship with him. It's a whole new perspective on being a father.

So this isn't a book written by a father who has no relationship with his kids. It is written by a son whose father is his hero and best friend and who wants that same kind of relationship with his own children. I thank God for my dad, and I work hard at becoming as good a father as he is today.

I believe if you and I do everything in this book, one day your kids, too, will be saying, "My dad is my hero and my best friend."

CHAPTER 1

I REFUSE TO ASK FOR DIRECTIONS

When a father has no vision, the relationship he
desires with his family perishes…

Imagine with me, if you will, your vacation that you
have spent 351 days, 50 work weeks, or 2,000-plus
work hours earning. This is your vacation.

Vacation for you starts at four o'clock in the
morning because you have to beat traffic and make good
time. For whatever reason, maybe some God-given
instinct, your biggest concern in life right now is making
better time than any other man you know. For the next
three weeks, this incredible feat of prowess will be the
topic of conversation with every man you meet. "Yep. I
made the trip in three hours and nineteen minutes. I cut
three minutes off the trip by lightening the overall vehicle
weight by not wearing a belt, shoes, or underwear."

Actually, this is going to be my family vacation.
So bear with me and enjoy the ride!

Here we are getting ready for the week of relax-
ation we deserve. I start out by loading the car for the big
trip. (Sometimes I wonder if hell is an eternity in which

all the men do is pack the vehicles for all the women going to Heaven.) I know this packing extravaganza is going to be a long, hard process, so I decide to wear my belt, shoes, and underwear at least for the time being. My wife and best friend in this endeavor is my archenemy. She is the "force of evil" I am trying to overcome!

My beautiful wife has decided to pack light this year, so she only gives me three suitcases, two duffle bags, a makeup bag, snack bag, game bag, diaper bag, CD bag, video bag, beach bag, book bag, magazine bag, miscellaneous bag in case she needs a bag, and a bag to hold bags.

For our children, she has packed three suitcases, four duffle bags, a portable crib the size of a VW van, a bag of toys, three bags of trip activities, a suitcase full of extra diapers and wipes, a bag of stuff they never use even at home, much less on vacation, a cooler for snacks, a combo TV-VCR, and twenty-eight annoying kids' videos that I will have to listen to while driving. (After listening to these movies over and over again, I am convinced that Satan will have these movies playing in the background in hell!)

Oh, I almost forgot—my wife packed all of my luggage too—and she hands me the last item I will have to maneuver into our vehicle: one small Green Bay Packers duffle bag that my parents gave me when I was eight.

My job now is to put 180 cubic feet of cargo into a space that holds 36 cubic feet. But this a dad can do! We may not be able to get a diaper on nice and tight, or feed the baby without food ending up on the walls—or watch the kids without some emergency task force being called to the house—but we have been given an extra chromosome (the "packasome") just for this kind of problem!

In just under two hours, my personal best, I have packed the car.

As I load the children into the car, my wife begins to complain about how cramped the vehicle is and about how I should have packed it differently. Why don't you keep your big mouth closed? I think, and I respond, "You're right, Dear. Guess I was just a little rushed. Next time, I will take my time and think things through."

Finally, everyone is buckled in. I sit down, put the key in the ignition, and my wife says, "Oh, no. I forgot my bag on the kitchen counter!" I think to myself, we're going to have to leave a child behind to get another bag in here!

In the early years of your marriage, when your wife said something like this, you probably thought she meant that she would get the bag since it was—after all—her bag, and she was the one who forgot it. But now that you've been married for a while, you understand that

I think to myself, We're going to have to leave a child behind to get another bag in here!

you must translate every word of your beloved's unique style of communication. For example: "I forgot my bag on the counter" might be "code talk" for, "Why did you let me forget my bag, you idiot! Go get it if you expect any chance of getting lucky tonight!"

In my case, I go into the house, get the bag, and curiously look inside to see what necessities of life we had almost forgotten. My jaw drops at the horror! It is her scrapbook bag—complete with four books, a bulky paper cutter, seventeen types of scissors, half a ream of assorted papers, and about a thousand pictures she will never ever get to!

On a side note, I believe this scrapbooking activity also came from the bowels of hell! It was designed to suck money and time from your wife. My wife can spend $30 and seventeen hours on one page containing one photograph and four hand-drawn, hand-colored, and hand-cut bees with the phrase "I Beez Cute." My mother could put 300 pictures in two cheap photo albums in seventeen minutes. But in one of my son's nine years and 4,000 pictures here on earth, my wife has only managed to "scrapbook" up to his first birthday!

Dutifully, I throw my wife's "scrap-o-rama" bag over my shoulder and, back at the car, finally wedge it under my three-year-old, convincing him that it's a pillow. Then backing out of the driveway, luggage, kids, and scrapbook bag in tow, I hear my son say, "Dad! I have to go…" (You fill in the blank, but I can guarantee you know the answer.)

I place the car in park and make the official bathroom announcement to all: "IF YOU HAVE TO GO TO THE BATHROOM, GO NOW! I WILL NOT BE STOPPING FOR ANOTHER FIVE HUNDRED MILES!" After every child has made a trip to the bathroom, off we go.

Seven minutes into our long-awaited journey, a small scuffle breaks out in the back seat over which video we will be playing first—on what, if you'll remember, was supposed to be my vacation, too.

At this point, my chest begins to tighten and my breathing becomes labored. Something snaps inside my very soul, and with my fingers clenching the steering wheel, like a madman, I whip the car across three lanes of traffic to the bicycle lane. I stop the car and make the official "let-the-vacation-begin" announcement: "IF I HEAR ONE MORE PEEP OUT OF ANYONE, I WILL TURN THIS CAR AROUND AND GO HOME!"

This is when my wife looks over at me and, with a sense of gentle curiosity in her voice, says, "So what got you in such a bad mood?"

If you're a father, I know you can relate to my exaggerated, yet not entirely unrealistic, account of the rigors of taking a family trip! But now imagine with me that, after all of this, you begin your vacation only to realize you have indeed forgotten to plan the one thing necessary for a successful trip: your destination.

"Where are you going?" someone asks. And you have to reply, "I don't know."

Think about it. Without an intended destination, how do you know if you're going in the right direction? And how do you know when you've arrived?

Of course, you understand that you can't begin a trip without a destination, without having some goal or vision, if you will, as to where you will end up. Without a vision, you will never arrive! And you will have no idea as to how to prepare.

A Vision for Fathering

It is the same with fatherhood. Many fathers leave on the "trip" of fathering (and it is a trip!) without having any idea where they're going. They have no real vision for fathering. Sure, they want their kids to grow up well and be successful, but just having that as a goal is as vague as my saying, "I want to go somewhere warm and sunny on my vacation!"

Think about this. What you pack and how you prepare for your vacation depends on where you're going. All of your planning, including the maps you'll take, the amount of money you'll need, and so forth, depends on your intended destination. You can't get there if you don't know where "there" is.

In much the same way, many fathers get excited about the new baby, and they jump in the car of life, speeding ahead toward what they think is the land of great fathering. The problem is, they don't know where "it" is. So they find themselves backtracking and feeling frustrated until they finally give up on their desire to be a great father and settle for just being a father.

The simple truth of the matter is this: Without vision, you will not be able to be a great father.

Nearly every book on leadership or success stresses the importance of having a vision for whatever you are doing. I read a great book once that said, "Where there is no vision, the people perish…" Dreams, aspirations, and the desires of your heart, including your desire to be a great father, perish without vision. Another translation: "Where there is no vision, the people are unrestrained."

Vision brings parameters, borders and boundaries into your life. With vision, you have controls that keep you moving toward the fulfillment of your vision. That vision guards and protects your desire, because it brings restraint into your life that won't allow you to do anything that would interfere with that desire coming to pass.

The opposite of that is true, too. When you lack vision, you lack the controls or restraints you need to

The simple truth of the matter is this: Without vision, you will not be able to be a great father.

13

move you toward your desire. You have no parameters in place to protect what you're desiring.

For example, most of us can remember a time when we really wanted something in life. Maybe it was a special bike, game, pocketknife, or even a car or house. Up until the time of that desire, perhaps we couldn't save a dime. We had no restraints in our lives where saving money was concerned. But then we got a vision. That vision would not allow us to waste our money. That vision may have caused us to work extra hours or take on another job. Our vision had so much power that it drove us toward the desire of our heart and would not let up until we had whatever it was we wanted.

Vision is one of the most powerful forces given to us. People often confuse vision with desire, but the two are distinctly different.

Desire is simply something you want. Vision is something you will have.

Desire is something you need. Vision is something you can't live without.

Desire will give you something to think about. Vision will give you something to live for!

A vision for great fathering won't allow you to invest your time in things that will take time away from your children. For example, you may want to spend another night in front of the TV just as you've been doing for who knows how long. But when you get a vision for great fathering, that vision will not allow you to do that. Your vision will push you toward putting forth the effort and hard work it takes to be a great dad. Your vision will not allow you to ignore your children's needs. It will not permit you to make empty promises. It will not allow you to stop growing and changing as a father. It will continually push you toward being the father you desire to be.

Let's apply this same truth to women in the area of weight-loss. (Since I'm writing this for men, I hope I can trust you not to tell any woman you know—or don't know, for that matter—that I included this in the book!) Let's say that a wife is struggling with her weight. She wants to lose weight, but she just can't seem to do it. Her metabolism or her genetic makeup just won't allow it!

Now, I'm no scientist, but maybe it's the buttered popcorn, nachos, and candy she scarfs down at the movie theatre. Or maybe it's all those fast-food meals she super-sizes that have caused her to be super-sized!

No, on second thought, that's probably not it; I'm probably wrong. In fact, I'm sure it was the DNA thing that did it. (I am speaking facetiously.)

Then suppose the marriage, for whatever reason, goes to divorce court. In seemingly no time at all, just in a couple of months, she drops thirty or forty pounds and is looking good!

What happened? Did her metabolism miracu-
lously change? Did the divorce papers change her
DNA? No, of course not. She went past desire and
got to vision. She wanted another husband, wanted her
ex-husband to want her back, or just wanted to prove
something to herself. To do that, she lost the weight.
The vision to lose weight was "birthed" inside of her,
and that vision brought restraints into her life. She
began refusing junk food, choosing to eat healthy foods
instead. She began working out consistently. Those op-
tions were always available to her; she just didn't know
how to tap into the power of vision.

Now let's apply the same truth to kids. If you
place vision in their hearts for something worthwhile,
you will watch them head toward success, fulfilling their
dreams and goals.

We can also see the power of vision in kids
keeping themselves sexually pure. Just telling kids that
premarital sex is bad will not keep their pants on. If anything, it will make it even more appealing. But what if
you put a vision for virginity into their hearts?

For example, tell your children what losing
their virginity steals from the one they will marry one
day. Explain to them the risks and the rewards. (If
you don't know the rewards, read some books on it.)
Put in their hearts the great things they can expect

when they follow the road less traveled. Then they will have the restraints in their lives that will not allow them to be with someone who is all wrong for them, someone who doesn't share their vision. Their vision will protect their desire.

If you put a vision within your children for hanging out with the right crowd, doing well in school, getting a college degree or some form of higher education, you will train them up in the way they should go, and that vision will steady and restrain them along life's path and not allow them to depart from it.

As dads, we sometimes need to be careful not to put too much vision into our kids. For example, my sons, Laken and Heath, were eight and seven, respectively, when I enrolled them both in gymnastics. Within two months, Heath was doing over twenty chin-ups and advancing to higher levels, while Laken could barely do one chin-up. I tried to get Laken to practice chin-ups every day, but he had no vision for it. So one day I said to him, "When you do fifteen chin-ups, I will buy you the new Game Boy you've been wanting."

I was expecting him to work on his chin-ups every day for a few months and then finally be able to do fifteen. But when I made that promise to him, he decided that "today" was the day he would go from one chin-up to fifteen!

~

We can also see the power of vision in kids keeping themselves sexually pure.

~

For five hours, Laken kept saying, "Dad, come outside and count." I'd answer, "Son, I already know the count. It's one."

"No, Dad, this time I will get it."

"No, Son, you won't. This is going to take a few months."

Well, that evening, Laken was still outside trying to do fifteen chin-ups. At eight o'clock, he came in and said, "Dad, I did it! I did fifteen chin-ups!"

I said, "Son, please don't lie to Dad. We both know you didn't do it."

He responded, "It wouldn't be a lie if you believed it."

That is quite a deep thought, I pondered. Maybe he'll run for public office someday.

On a serious note, real vision always brings parameters into your life that will guide you toward the fulfillment of your desire. You can't just have a desire for a certain outcome—even a strong desire. You have to have the vision for it, which brings with it the determination that you will have it.

Let's take his idea of vision a step further. Suppose you want to quit smoking. You desire it. You've set seemingly thousands of goals and have thrown your cigarettes away hundreds of times. You've thrown your smokes on the altar and then went home mad because you wasted three bucks worth of cigarettes! You've even had your pastor lay hands on you to cast out that "nicotine" demon!

You see, desires alone are not strong enough to overcome the habit. You need the power of vision. For some people, that vision will come when the doctor says, "If you don't quit smoking, you'll be dead in a year." Suddenly, vision is birthed, and they are now able to quit. That vision won't allow them to smoke. It is more powerful than their habit.

Do you know why extramarital affairs happen? A lack of vision. Where there is no vision, marriages perish. But vision will not allow you to have an affair. It doesn't matter how much your human nature wants to do it—vision will not allow it. Vision protects your desire to have a great marriage, a marriage that's "heaven on earth." That vision is stronger than any habit or desire of human nature. It won't matter that another woman is "hot"—your vision is hotter! The pull may be strong, but the vision is stronger.

Vision makes you talk to your wife after work when you really just want to watch TV. Vision makes you attend the marriage seminar when you want to stay home and watch TV. Vision makes you take your wife out on a nice date every single week when you would rather watch TV! Vision puts her needs above yours.

Your human nature is pulling you in the opposite direction, but your vision is stronger.

In many cases, the only thing missing in a marriage is vision. The husband and wife love each other, but they lack the vision they need to make the marriage everything they desire.

You see, a desire is something you hope for, but a vision is something you obtain. A desire only gives you thoughts of success, but a vision actually brings you toward that success. If you want to receive and enjoy the desires of your heart, you need vision. Vision will produce your desires.

This should excite you! Every one of us has desires, things we want in our lives. How do we get them? Vision. We want to be great fathers. How do we get there? Vision. We have to learn how to tap into the power of vision.

CHAPTER 2
THIS BOOK IS 'FINISHED,' AND 'IT IS GOOD!'

...Write the vision, and make it plain upon tables,
that he may run that readeth it.

L ast January I had surgery on my right knee. After
six months of rehab and exercise, I was going to
have a strength test performed on the knee. At that point,
I was excited, because if I passed this strength test and
my right leg was as strong as my left leg, I could play
sports again.

So I drive all the way out to Phoenix to this huge
gym, where the strength test will be performed. I walk
in the door and it is an amazing sight, because—and,
please, don't tell my wife—as far as the eye could see,
there are beautiful women. It's like the training center
for a college girls' volleyball team. (Correction: I am
only assuming they were beautiful, because I am married and did not look.)

Finally, I see the only guy in this gym, and he's
behind the desk. He's a surfer guy. I didn't know these
guys still existed, but there he is. He's unshaven and has
the long curly hair, the OP tank top, and the surfer shorts.

I walk up to him, and he says, "What's up, D..u..d..e?" with that long drawn-out surfer d…u…d…e.

I answer, "I'm here for my knee, (slight unsure pause) Dude." Then he says, "Cool, D..u..d..e. You, like, need to fill out some paperwork." I say, "Cool, Dude."

So I take the paperwork, fill it out and give it back to "Spicoli." He then brings out this very pretty lady (I assume she was pretty—didn't look). Michelle is going to do my training with me.

Now, realize that I have not done any exercise in a year except to go upstairs and go to bed. That has been the extent of my daily exercise program.

Michelle, "Little Miss Jane Fonda," decides to get me going on a "marathon." She puts the incline on the treadmill as high as it will go and gets me running, and running, and running. Finally, just before I was going to pass out, she says, "Good. We're done running." Oh, thank sweet Jesus, I think. Then she hands me a rope and says, "Let's jump." Then after what seems to be an eternity, she says, "Now let's jump from side to side; now let's jump high; now let's double jump…" Then, "Run in place." And after that, "Climb these steps one jillion times."

I don't exactly remember what happened next, but I think I began to cry like a little girl. I began to pray that Jesus would just take me right then. I'm crying out similar to how I picture Moses screaming out to Pharaoh

DAD

"LET MY PEOPLE GO!!!" I feel like I have endured all the plagues, and it is time to set me free.

Now that I can't move my leg, I am informed that we're ready to do the strength test.

Now remember, I want my right knee to be as strong as the left knee. If it is, I can play sports again. As we're doing the stretches and the leg curls, my knee is doing great. Finally, we get to the leg press. I push up 240 pounds three times with my left leg. Little Miss Fonda says, "Okay, now the right leg."

Please picture the scene with me. To my right are four pretty girls doing sit-ups (or something like that, because I didn't look). Then over to my left are a couple of girls passing a medicine ball back and forth. In front of me, there is a group of girls doing leg-extension exercises. And my training lady is right beside me. So within three feet of my world are about ten women. With everything in my very being, I begin pushing with the right leg. I want it to be strong, so I'm giving it everything I've got. Each time I push, I keep arching my back, and Little Jane keeps saying, "Stop arching your back. Let's try that again."

So here we go. I'm pushing with everything I've got, and I'm halfway there. I feel like the veins in my neck are going to burst. She cries out, "Stop arching your back!" And then she pushes on my stomach.

I don't exactly remember what happened next, but I think I began to cry like a little girl.

Now, you know, of course, that you don't ever, ever, ever push on a man's stomach while he is pushing anything, because if you do, he'll lose all control over what his body will do afterward. (They should teach women that in physical therapy school, don't you think? It should be Lesson 28 or something: "Don't push on a man's belly. If you do, this is what's going to happen, and it will make this kind of mess.")

So Jane pushes, and a noise sounds forth from my backside that could be heard for a city block: FHPPPH-GURGLEFHPPHGURGLEFHPPPHTH. It was the single worst fart I have ever passed in my life. There has been some fierce competition, but that one was the worst.

Little Jane's eyes look like they're going to pop out. Her mouth dropped, and I was speechless, afraid that I had blown the seat apart behind me. I turned to see if I had shot my spleen out somewhere. I think we were all surprised that the fire sprinklers didn't go off.

Everything in the gym stops. About forty girls stop what they're doing and look over at me. And why wouldn't they? They probably thought some terrorist act had occurred.

Time freezes. I'm just sitting there. In my mind, my life flashes before my eyes. I begin to ask God what to do. I think, Your Word has no instructions about this. Your Word is supposed to be for every circumstance, but there's nothing in there for this. I feel like You lied to me. A thought pops into my head that says, "Run, Man. Just run and never look back." But I can't run; my legs are too tired. Then a beautiful thought comes to mind: Blame it on Jane Fonda. That worked in junior high.

Just as I was about to say to her, "You're disgusting!" it was like God stepped in and answered my prayers. Everyone went back to doing what they were doing—like nothing even happened. Sure they'll all laugh later, I thought, but we're adults here. Let's just ignore it. But just then, from across the room, Surfer Boy cries out, "D..U..D..E! I heard that all the way over here, D.u.d.e!" Laughter erupts such as the earth has never heard. Grown women are rolling on the floor laughing so hard they can't breathe. My trainer drops to her knees and starts laughing uncontrollably.

For the remainder of the session, every time I walk by Surfer Boy, he has a funny little comment for me, like "Bro—you smell like corn nuts, Dude!"

It's funny things like this that happen to us in life that show us what things are unimportant in the scheme of things and what things are really important. Being embarrassed in front of a small army of Wonder Women is not very important, relatively speaking. Being a great father to my kids and having them be a part of my life until I pass from this life is very, very important.

To achieve this goal of great fathering takes more than six months of intensive training and exercise. It takes a lifestyle of building relationships. Where do we begin? The obvious answer is from the moment your kids are born. But assuming you haven't always done the right thing because you haven't known what to do, we'll start with your vision for being a great father.

'Finishing' Before You Start

An important part of having a vision for great fathering is writing down your vision. But a key part of writing a vision is finishing it before you start it. For example, when you're planning a vacation, you "finish" the vacation before you start it. You plan where you'll be going, how long you'll be gone, where you'll stay, what you need to pack, how much money you'll need, and so forth. Once it is finished, then you start it.

Similarly, to be a great father, you have to finish being a great father so you can start being a great father.

If you and I are going to have a vision, we must develop this skill of "finishing before we start"—this quality of seeing it before it happens. We already do this in various ways every day. For example, we see dinner done before we cook it. We see our house built before the contractors start building it.

DAD

To build a house, you don't just start throwing walls up. You have to have detailed plans written down. You have to have a plan as to where every wire and outlet will be placed, where all the pipes will be installed, and so forth. Once you have all the plans, the house is "finished." Then you start to build it. If you start building it before your plans are finished, the outcome could be disastrous (I think that's the first time I've ever used that word). For example, you might pour concrete and then realize you need plumbing. So you have to tear up the concrete, put in the plumbing, and redo the concrete. Then, oops, you forgot the plumbing for yet another bathroom, so you tear it up one more time.

Without written plans, you would be constantly tearing up what you've already done in order to fix problems. This describes life for some people. They start something—in the way of disciplining their children, for example—and then, oops, they forgot something, and they have to start all over. They have to rethink the whole thing. They'll say, "Well, that doesn't work. Let's try this." Then if that doesn't work, they try this and this and this. Had they "finished" it before they started it, they wouldn't have had to keep going back and starting over.

If you don't finish your vision—if you don't know where you're going—you're going to be constantly backtracking, throwing away what you've been working on.

> You have to finish being a great father so you can start being a great father.

"What if I finish it wrong?" someone asks.

Let's say that you're on your way to San Diego, and there is a detour that you didn't know about. Your directions showed no indication of a detour. Does that mean that it is futile to write directions and plot your course?

No, of course not! Under that type of thinking, you would never write down directions because there might be a detour along the way. But you would be planning for failure if you did that. No, you finish your trip, and then you start your trip. And if there happens to be an unexpected detour, you flow with it.

Things will change in life, but you have to have a vision and then just flow with the change. Concerning fatherhood, you have to finish it, start it, and be able to flow with change if it comes. In other words, it is important that your vision remains finished but that you be flexible.

My father always said it is impossible to steer a bicycle that isn't moving. How true that is concerning our lives. It is impossible to get anywhere if you don't start moving.

So, together, let's "finish" our children right now, so we can start our journey to being great fathers.

In a sense, I am finishing this book in this one chapter. I am setting forth and finishing the vision on which the rest of the chapters will be built. Once I finish this, I can write the rest. In this chapter, I will show you my vision for great fathering. As you read it, feel free to take with you those things you want to see at the end of your own journey.

First, the obvious things I want my children to have are good habits. Now, we tend to think of a habit in terms of a bad habit, something we want to quit doing, but we can develop good habits, too. In fact, I believe that habits are something given to us to help us become successful. If I train certain habits into the hearts of my children, when they get old, they will not depart from them.

For example, my children will have a habit of growing, changing, and becoming better in life. They grow to be adults who are striving to be a better spouse, better in their profession, better in life. These things become habits. Then, even though they might want to just stay the same, they can't, because this habit will be hard to break.

I also want my children to have a habit of loving others. They may want to be mean or not want to love. But they can't, because of this habit of loving others that's inside them. Then one day, when marriage gets a little tough and those around them say, "Just give up," they won't, because they'll have the habit of love and dedication. That habit will push them toward attending marriage seminars and reading books on the subject of marriage. That habit will eventually drive them into having an amazing marriage.

My children will also have a habit of not giving up. When others have quit and walked away from their dreams, my children will have a habit of persevering, of giving their all. This habit will lead them into a habit of success. Even if they wanted to be unsuccessful, they couldn't, because of this unbreakable habit of persevering.

They will have a habit of being happy. They may want to join the other eighty percent of the world that can find unhappiness in anything, but they will choose to look at the good things in life. They will see problems as nothing more than opportunities to grow and change—as challenges to be conquered. They will see every day as a great day. They will expect the best out of life. The interesting thing is, whatever you expect, you almost always get.

So my first vision for my children is good habits. My second vision is at the heart of this book. It is one of my greatest desires for them, and also that when they grow up, they have with me what my dad and I have today—friendship.

The Heart of the Vision

My dad and I have a great friendship and relationship. To me, my relationship with my kids is vitally important, too. I don't want them to grow up, move away, call me on the holidays, and see me twice a year. Of course, I want my kids to be successful in all that they do, but I also want them to be my best friends, just as my father is my best friend.

I want my kids to look forward to spending time with me. I want time with Dad to be something they are excited about doing, not something they have to do. I want them to honor me because they want to, not because they have to. I want them to love talking to me because of what we have together as friends— not feel as though they have to talk to me so I won't cut them out of the will! I've heard many fathers say, "I hope I don't turn out like my father." I work hard at trying to become just like mine. I want my children to say the same thing about me.

Notice how I'm setting a much different goal for fathering than society has set. I say that fathering is about developing a relationship with my children. Society says that fathering is to provide for and to protect your children. These two goals will result in two different destinations. On my way to relationship, I will pass through providing for and protecting my children, but my destination will be different. My vision goes way beyond society's vision for great fathering.

At the end of life, doesn't society judge fathers solely on how well they provided and protected? People will say, "He was a great dad. He always put food on the table and a roof over their heads." Nobody mentions that he perhaps hadn't talked to his children in ten years and some of them didn't even go to the funeral! But in society's eyes, he was considered a great dad. Many would say, "The kids were just spoiled." But, listen, things only spoil when they're put in the wrong environment. If the kids are spoiled, Dad failed as a father.

I believe that a father who only provided for and protected his kids fulfilled the role of a father, all right, but he fell way short of being a great dad. He failed to develop and nurture a relationship with them. The things he provided for his kids could not take the place of having a relationship with them.

In this book, I'm saying that there is a higher level of fathering that is based on the relationship between father and child. This relationship is the vision, the "finished product" that a great father strives to see fulfilled.

As I said, the world says that a father must provide and protect to be a great father. That's good, but I want more. I want my children still coming to me for advice and still wanting to spend time with me when they are in their twenties and older. I want to have a great relationship with all of my children, a relationship that just keeps getting better our whole lives. And one day, when I'm 120 and I pass from this earth, my children will say, "There lies my father and my best friend. We shared many years of great memories together!"

Do you see how a vision is finished now? With that in mind, how does that change what you do as a father today? Do you see the power of vision? Your vision for being a great father will change who you are and who you become to your children. It will change the time you spend with them, but more importantly, it will change the kind of time you spend with them.

The Focus of Our Vision:
Spending Time or Building Relationships?

I'm sure we all have heard the terms "quality time" and "quantity time," and we've heard it said, "It's not the quantity of time you spend with your children, but the quality of time you spend with them." More often than not, this is quoted as some lame excuse a dad uses to soothe his conscience. Dads will spend seven hours of quantity time with the television, and then thirty minutes of so-called quality time with their kids. "But it was quality time," they'll say. Really? What made it quality time?

When you talk about quantity of time and quality of time, what is the focus? Time! Both are time-centered. If your vision is to spend quality time with your children, you have a vision, or destination, that is focused on time rather than on relationship. Time becomes the priority; time is first, relationship-building is second. In other words, your children's needs are bound to time rather than your time being bound to their needs!

Spending quality and quantity time with our children is very important. We need to do that. But if you're using time to determine whether you're a good father or not, at the end of life, you will come up short of your vision of having a close friendship with your kids.

Many fathers who have no relationship with their children today played catch with their kids, had tea parties with their daughters, and took their kids to the park. Those are great activities, but the fathers who did these things and didn't build a relationship with their kids just took twenty minutes out of their day to play catch or have tea and cookies so they could feel good about how they were doing as a dad. During that time, the relationship didn't really grow.

Sometimes dads, out of their competitive nature, try to make their kid the next Nolan Ryan, and light into the child for not focusing or not practicing enough. They're spending time with him, but the relationship is not growing. They have a tea party with their daughter, but their mind is on the football game or on work, and no real conversation takes place during the time spent. The relationship doesn't grow. They go to the park with their kids, and the kids play while dad sits on the bench and does some work. They're spending time, but no relationship-building is taking place.

Do you see how time can become the goal instead of relationship? There are a lot of fathers and children out there who can't stand each other, but who spent time together as the children were growing up. My father told me some time ago not to grade myself as a father on the quality and quantity of time I spend with my child, but on the quality and quantity of the relationship that comes out of the time I spend with him or her.

Time is important but it's not our goal. When having a relationship with your kids is your goal, it will change how you spend your time with them. A frustrating time of playing catch with Dad as he tries to make his child into a great pitcher suddenly becomes a relaxing time of throwing the ball and sharing hopes and dreams with Dad. A time of listening to Dad talk on the cell phone while he pushes his child on the swing turns into a time of his child opening up and sharing what's going on inside of her while Dad pushes her on the swing.

Time is important but it's not our goal.

We are on our way to great fathering when we no longer measure how good a father we are by the amount of time we spend with our children or by how well we provide for and protect them. We measure our fathering skills by the relationship that we have built and are continuing to build with our children. If you and I can build the friendship and relationship with our kids that my own father built with me, I believe we will have fulfilled our role as a father.

Relationship is the vision. Now let's start building.

CHAPTER 3

DAD, ARE YOU SURE THIS BRIDGE WILL HOLD ME?

Here we are at LEGOLAND, and my family and I have been waiting for the last thirty minutes to meet my parents, who left at the exact same time. Understand that we both have global positioning systems in our vehicles, which, by the way, is quite possibly the greatest invention of all time. (And the GPS lady's voice is so sexy—I love it when my wife talks to me like the GPS lady!).

Like I said, my parents have the GPS, so getting to LEGOLAND should be very simple. At that moment, my cell phone rings and my mom starts telling me the GPS doesn't work. I can hear my dad in the background, yelling, "I will rip this system out of the car and throw it in the ocean! I will never buy a vehicle with a GPS again!"

Please understand that my parents are "technologically challenged." My dad's cell phone, on which we spent countless hours trying to teach him how to check his messages, now has a recording of me that says, "Please don't leave a message, because my father, who can rebuild a Chevy 350 engine from the ground up, can't remember how to check his messages!"

So my mom is saying, "This thing doesn't work."

And I'm telling her, "All you do is type in 'LE-GOLAND,' and it works."

I can hear my mom telling my dad, "Tom, that's not how you spell LEGO. It's not L-O-G-O Land—it's L-A-G-O!"

Now that's funny, but sometimes the process of becoming a great dad is just like that.

We already "finished" being a great dad—in other words, we see the end result. Now we can start becoming a great dad. We have our destination; now we need our map. We need to know how to get there. We need to plug it into the GPS of life.

But first, let's find out where you are. Some dads may be well on their way toward a great relationship with their children, while others are wandering around in the land of having children who say, "I can't stand my father!"

I have read books and listened to tapes that have had thousands of questions designed to determine what kind of father you are. But I have just one question. And the answer to this one question will tell you where you are right now and then point you toward where you need to be.

To find out where you are on the "fathering" scale, all you have to do is answer the question: "Do my children trust me?" Whether they are five years old or forty, do your children trust you?

DAD

Building Trust Through Building Relationships

I am thinking about this very question when Baylor, my four-year-old, asks me to push him on his swing. As I am pushing him, I begin to think that right now in his life, he trusts everything I say. If I were to say the sky is green and the grass is blue, he would believe me.

Baylor doesn't doubt my love or commitment. In his heart, he believes that Dad can do and fix anything. There is no problem, no situation, no mountain too big for Dad—nothing that Dad can't conquer.

Right now, Baylor knows that unconditional love can be found by simply walking over to Dad and getting a hug. Security is just a bedroom away from where he sleeps. Acceptance is found in Dad's arms. Help is just a scream away. Finding happiness is as easy as saying, "Dad, will you push me on the swing?" Right now, everything is a little bit better when Dad is around.

I'll tell you an embarrassing story to show you just how much your children will believe everything you tell them. Last week, I introduced the classic game of "pull my finger" into Baylor's life.

This is one game I swore I would never play with my children, possibly because of all the "fun-filled" hours I had spent playing it with my dad. But for whatever reason, I felt that this nurturing game was a must in my young son's life. So I said, "Come here and pull Dad's

> Baylor knows that unconditional love can be found by simply walking over to Dad and getting a hug.

finger." Naturally, he did what I told him to. He pulled my finger, and—well, you know what happened next. At that moment, I became the funniest person in the world to my son. (I wish comedy were that easy—I would be on the "Pull My Finger" comedy tour!)

The next day at church, in the middle of the foyer and in front of a bunch of people, Baylor cries out, "Watch, Mom!" He walks over to me, and I'm wondering what in the world he's doing. He grabs my finger and starts to pull. He keeps pulling, and then he walks around behind me before he finally looks at me and says, "Dad, your tooter is broke!"

You see, at age four, children believe whatever you say. They trust their parents. But one day Baylor will be thrown out into the real world. He will learn that you can't trust everyone. There are those out in the world who take rather than give, who hurt rather than love. There are those in the world who will not accept Baylor for who he is. But his dad isn't one of those people.

Baylor will have plenty of relationship disappointments in his life—friends who will stab him in the back, bosses who will treat him unfairly, women who will break his heart. There will be many people in Baylor's life who will not be trustworthy. But guess what? I won't be one of them.

That day on the swings, I made a commitment that Baylor would never have a reason to doubt me. Twenty years from now, I want Baylor to know that security is just one phone call away. Acceptance is still found in Dad's arms. And finding happiness is as easy as saying, "Hey, Dad, let's hang out today." Twenty years from now, I want everything to still be a little bit better when Dad is around.

Baylor—and all of my children—will always know that no matter what happens in life, Dad will be there to love, accept, help, and guide them. This is a life-long commitment. There is no point at which I can stop growing or can assume that my behavior doesn't matter.

Trust is something I hope Baylor will never have to question, because I will do everything in my power to assure him that I'm still the same man he looked up to at four years old. When he's older, I want him to still be able to trust everything I say and have no question of my love. I want him to believe that unconditional love can still be found in a hug from Dad.

That is where I stand on the issue of trust. Now, be honest: Where are you on the issue? Do your children really trust you? "Sure, they trust me," you may say. To be sure, ask yourself, "Who do they go to when they have a problem, need something, or want advice?" Do they listen to you and trust what you have to say? If not, then you are lying to yourself.

You may wonder why trust is so important. It's important because it is the foundation of any relationship. No relationship will ever go beyond the level of trust. This applies to friendship, marriage, parenting—every relationship. If your trust level with someone is a two, then your relationship will never go beyond that level. How can you open up and share your dreams, desires, aspirations, and goals with someone you can't trust? Why go to someone for advice if you don't trust what he has to say?

Think about your own life. Think about someone who lied to you, broke trust with you, and then wanted to take the relationship to the next level. It couldn't happen—not until trust was reestablished.

The relationship is the house you build, while trust is the foundation. If the foundation is weak, the relationship will crumble, no matter how much time you put into it. You could be the nicest, funniest dad in the world. You could play ball with your children, buy them everything they want, and tell them the best jokes (I suggest the "pull-my-finger" joke). But if your kids can't trust you, all that time is wasted. No joke can overcome broken trust, and no amount of time spent together can build a relationship on a foundation of broken trust. Remember, time isn't the goal; relationship is. And to build a relationship, you must have a foundation of trust.

Learning To Fly

Trust isn't solely about building relationships. Having your children trust your word can save their lives. It can keep them from making huge mistakes. Sure, when your kids are little, they obey you because they have to. But sometimes in the teen years, they obey you because they trust you.

Raising kids is like teaching someone how to fly. In the beginning, the instructor sits right there next to you and can grab the wheel if you don't listen to the instructions or even land the plane if you get into trouble. But there comes a time when you are on your own, and the only advice you receive from your instructor is from the tower over the radio. Now whether or not you listen to the advice is determined by the level of trust you have in your instructor's words.

It's the same with children. When they're six years old, for example, you are right there next to them, ready to take that "wheel" if they get into trouble. You'll even land the plane if you have to! But then one day, those kids are in junior high and high school, and you are sitting out in the tower giving advice. "Don't hang around that crowd!" "Don't do drugs!" "Work hard in school!" "Go to college!"

But now that child has the choice to listen or not. Does he trust Dad's advice enough to listen? Or maybe

> The relationship is the house you build, while trust is the foundation.

his own desires or his friends' advice seems more trust-worthy. Many teenagers have crashed the plane of life because Dad's words didn't ring true in their minds.

I don't know about you, but I want my children to trust me. I want them at age fifteen still coming to me for advice. Though they might not agree with what I tell them to do, I want them to trust me enough to still do it.

Advice From the Wisest of Fathers

As I said before, trust will determine to whom your children will come for advice when they have a problem. Do they go to the world or to Dad? Their trust in you will be the determining factor.

As fathers, how many times do we say, "If only my kids would listen to me—if they would just listen to my advice. I know what I'm talking about! Why won't they listen to me?" The reason is simple: The relation-ship lacks trust.

You say to your children that premarital sex isn't right, but their friends and the world say there is nothing wrong with it. Whose advice do they trust? If the words of your daughter's boyfriend sound more true than yours, she could end up in the backseat of his car.

You say, "Don't drink. Don't do drugs. They're dangerous addictions." But your kids' friends and Rapper "Big Bootie Two Crap" say, "There's nothing wrong with it. It's an awesome high." Whose advice do they trust? If their friends' advice sounds more true than yours, then alcohol and drugs will become a part of their lives.

What your kids do when you're not around is determined by the level of trust in you that you have instilled in their hearts.

Doing What's Best for Others Builds Trust

As fathers, we need to have a mindset of building trust. In everything we do, our hearts should be in this trust-building mode. We need to have hearts for what is best for our kids—not what is best for us.

Think about it. If you have some money and want someone to take care of it for you, you don't trust someone who's looking for what's best for him. You want someone who wants what is best for you, someone who invests your money and makes money for you. And when that investor makes the investments that are best for you, over time, it builds a stronger and stronger trust between the two of you. But if he starts making deals that are simply best for him, that trust is destroyed.

The same is true concerning the father-child relationship. A father who makes decisions based on what is best for himself will slowly tear down whatever trust he and the child have. But a father whose decisions are best for the child will build a trusting relationship with those decisions.

Trust Is the Bridge

What is trust? To me, trust is a bridge built between two people that allows each to cross over safely into the other person's world.

Sure, many dads can see their kids' world—they can watch from a distance but they are unable to cross over because of a poorly built bridge. They might be able to see their child heading down a wrong path. They can scream out across the bridge but it doesn't matter. The child can't hear his father or doesn't want to hear him.

I want my children to feel like they can cross the bridge anytime for any need. My attitude is, "Please come into my world for anything at all. And please, allow me to speak into your world."

You see, for most kids, the bridge is old, worn out, and very shaky. On that first step across, a board may break underneath them. Maybe they came to Dad with a problem one time, and Dad blew up at them: "How could you even think about doing that?" Maybe Dad doesn't have time, and crossing the bridge isn't worth a child's effort. Maybe Dad never keeps his word. Because the child has no confidence in the bridge, he will not risk crossing it. He feels that chances are the bridge will break underneath him. Chances are he will take the long way and not go to Dad at all.

What would compel a child to try and cross the bridge into your world? An extreme emergency when he had to cross? Is that what you want? Or do you want your bridge to be strong so that your children never even question whether it will hold them. Anytime, anywhere, they know without a doubt, they can safely cross that bridge.

When it comes to your future relationship with your children, the bottom line is this: If a child can't trust you any more than his friends, then his friends, not you, will shape his destiny.

What kind of relationship do you have with your kids? Is it built on trust? Who will your children believe—you or some outside influence? On the road-map of life, do you know where you are? You do if you understand that on the roadmap of the relationship you have with your children, trust is one of the first and most important stops on your way to becoming a great dad.

~
Trust is a bridge built between two people that allows each to cross over safely into the other person's world.
~

CHAPTER 4

IT'S TIME YOU PUT YOUR WIFE IN HER PLACE

Here I am on the third day of watching the kids by myself. Not having slept in three days (since I stay up playing video games all night when Holly's gone), I am almost out of my wits. It is 8:35 a.m., and Laken starts kindergarten at 8:30. (Why this five year-old can't be more responsible is beyond me.) As I am rushing to get the kids into the van, Laken grabs an Avon® catalog off the driveway. He says, "Dad, can I read this?"

"Okay," I answer hurriedly. In my day, an Avon® catalog just had makeup in it—maybe a few pretty girls modeling their blush or mascara—the worst-case scenario being a close-up photo of women's lips.

So my mind, having gotten only two hours of sleep the night before, quickly computes the information: No harm; it will keep him quiet. And I blurt out, "Yes, Son, you may read it."

Off we go to Laken's school, one that some might call a strict school of a certain denomination in which most everything in life is deemed as evil. Mind you, it is a very good school academically, one of the best in our state, but their biblical views are a little different from mine.

I remember once, more recently, getting a call from Laken's second-grade teacher saying she was very, very concerned. I'm thinking, What did Laken do? Did he hit someone? Cuss? My goodness, is he smoking again? (That is a joke.)

The tone of this teacher's voice made it sound to me like Laken was into some life-destroying habit. She says, "Today, Laken... (there is a long, uncomfortable pause)..." Now, I'm really starting to be concerned. I'm thinking, Okay, what word did he say? Sh@#? Damn? Maybe the scriptural term for donkey? Whatever it is, this is big. I squirm a little, waiting for her to articulate Laken's dark sin. Finally, she stutters, "He said poop. Laken said poop."

Holy sh@#! No way! I will beat his biblical don-key! (Again, that is a joke.) I finally respond with, "We will deal with that."

Understand I'm not saying that poop is appro-priate. I am saying that we blew the situation way out of proportion.

I shared that to show you how strict a school this is. Again, I love the school. It's a great school. It's just a very strict school.

Now back to Laken's being late to kindergar-ten (his teacher, by the way, is the daughter of the church's pastor).

I should have known something was wrong because the kids were giggling during the whole trip to school. So I drop Laken off at school and take the two youngest kids home for naptime. At noon, we take off again to pick Laken up. As I'm driving, I can hear, from the back of the van, Heath, who was four at the time, giggling in a sinister tone. Actually, his laugh sounded similar to that of "Beavis": "Hrrr...rrr...rr."

We get to the school. I get Baylor and I say, "Come on, Heath, get out of the van," at which time Heath responds, "Dad, look!" He then shows me a picture from this "makeup" catalog of a half-dressed woman in lingerie. He laughs again: "Hrrr...rrr...rr."

"Oh my gosh!!!" I say as I snatch the catalog out of his hands. I cry out with all that is within me, "HEATH, YOU DON'T LOOK AT GIRLY MAGAZINES!"

"Why not, Dad?" Heath asks.

"You just don't do it. No, no, no!"

"But, Dad, it was at our house," he says. "I know that, Son, but this magazine is for big people to read." Heath thinks for a moment and says, "So you can read it, right, Dad?"

"Yes, Son, Daddy can read this."

He accepts this answer and off we go to Laken's classroom. Outside the classroom are all the other parents, many of whom attend my church. The students

> His laugh sounded similar to that of "Beavis."

are getting their backpacks on to go home. Laken is toward the back of the classroom. Out of nowhere, Heath screams out, "LAKEN!" I look at Heath curiously, wondering what in the world he's doing.

Laken screams back, "WHAT!" and Heath screams, "DAD SAYS WE CAN'T LOOK AT THE GIRLY MAGAZINE ANYMORE!!!"

My jaw drops. Everyone turns and looks at us—kind of in slow motion. I look from face to face at the looks of shock and horror and I'm thinking Why me, Lord? Just then, Heath screams out again, "DAD SAYS ONLY HE CAN LOOK AT THE GIRLY MAGAZINE!!!"

There were gasps from the crowd, and some parents pulled their kids close to them, as if I was some kind of "sick-o" that might snatch them and run. At this point, I conclude that there is no way to explain what just happened. I have no words to offer. As everyone stares at the "perv" and his children, we just walk away as, all the while, Laken is insisting, "But, Dad, you said I could look at it!"

"Yes, Son, you're right. I did say that," I answer as I vow that I will never let Holly go anywhere ever again. And that's what I want to talk about in this chapter: putting your wife in her place.

"You are the most insensitive slob, and I don't know what I ever saw in you!" my normally adoring wife Holly screamed at me. "You never listen to me. You never…," and she proceeded to launch into a whole bunch of stuff that I tuned out.

Being the man of character that I was those many, many years ago, I responded, "Coming from someone who lies around the house all day, that doesn't hurt my feelings so much. Maybe I wouldn't be so insensitive— maybe I would find one thing you say interesting—if you gave me a little more—let's just say—'attention'!"

I had done it. I had played the sex card—that secret weapon I keep in my back pocket and only bring out when I really want to turn up the heat. Holly burst out in tears, and as sad as this sounds, it felt good. (Now, being a man of character and a person who's always trying to grow and become better, it is confusing to me why this brought so much joy to me. But it was a triumphant moment in my life. I'd won. I emerged the grand champion of the fight, proving once again that I have the ability to hurt my best friend and love of my life. And my reward? No 'attention' that night.)

Just then Laken, my oldest son, who was three at the time, walked in and, in an angry voice, said, "You stop being mean to my mom!"

I thought, Me? Mean? Did you not hear the first twenty minutes of her telling me how worthless I am? Did you not hear the millions of things she said about me! She said a hundred mean things to my one!

It was at this point that I realized how important it is that I treat Mom right. Whether Mom is right or wrong—nice or not—it doesn't matter. Children want their dad to love their mom.

To be a great father, the most important thing you can do is love the mother of your children. In fact, this is one of the best ways to start building that trust with your children.

Understand that in this chapter, I am speaking to men who are married to their children's mothers and to men who are not. It is a very difficult chapter to write and maybe more difficult to read if you are divorced. You must take into account what applies to your situation, realizing that condemnation isn't the purpose here. Condemnation will never produce anything good. Instead, let's learn to be the best dads we can from that perspective.

Of course, it is easier and better for the children if Mom and Dad are married. That is just a fact: Mom and Dad together is the best-case scenario. But that doesn't mean you can't raise great kids and have a great relationship with them if you're divorced. It just means more work because trust has been broken. Rather than continuing to break the trust, you can build it. The extra work it takes will be well worth the effort.

As a single dad, you will nullify all of your good intentions and hard work with your children if you talk badly about their mother and don't love her unconditionally—not based on what she does or doesn't do, but because she exists. If for no other reason, you love her because she is the most important and influential woman in your children's lives. In this, you know that love conquers all. She may talk badly about you to the kids. But you stay your course and speak only positively about her. One day, the truth will be revealed to the kids.

As a divorced father, you should back your ex-wife up on the things she wants done with the kids. You make sure the kids respect and honor her. Teach your children to love their mom. In doing these things, you are building trust in your children, but you are also building trust in her. So when the time comes, and you and your ex don't agree on a particular parenting direction, it is the love you have given that will give you a window, an opening, to speak into her life. Over time, your love will build a trust within her that you do have the best interests of your children at heart. It will be this trust that, although you are divorced, will still allow you to guide and steer the family toward what is best for the children.

Besides, whatever the case, whatever the details of the divorce, leave the past where it belongs, behind you. There is a reason why the windshield of a car is

~

You love her because she is the most important and influential woman in your children's lives.

~

so much bigger than the rear view mirror; we should spend a lot more time focusing on what is ahead of us, rather than what is behind us.

First Things First

Now, the first thing you need to do to build a trusting relationship with your children is to love your children's mom.

Think of it from a child's perspective: How much trust can he have in a father who talks down to his mom, who is rude to her, and who speaks negatively about her? How much trust can that child have in a father who is not gentle with his mother, who does not value her? How much trust can he have in a father who does things behind his mother's back, a father who doesn't back her up but only puts her down? How can a child trust a man who does not love the most important woman in that child's life?

All the fun time you spend with your kids and all your hard work to be a great father is wasted if you're not a great husband first (or loving her as an ex). You cannot be a great dad unless you are a great husband—or, for single dads, you cannot be a great dad unless you love your children's mother.

The Security of a Solid Marriage

As I said, you cannot be a great father until you are a great husband. This means that the husband-wife relationship has to be the priority relationship of the family. It is the heart of the family; it is what the children draw their security from. If the husband-wife relationship is not secure, the children will be insecure. Remember, we're still talking about trust—and insecurity is the opposite of trust. One way to instill security is by letting your kids know your marriage is secure.

If kids go off to school and in their hearts they have no doubt of Mom and Dad's love for each other, imagine their sense of security. They know that divorce is never an option, that their mom and dad will do anything to work things out even if they do fight once in a while. Guess what? With that worry off their shoulders, kids can focus on school, friends, and being a kid. They can go forth confidently into the world.

But what if Mom and Dad are constantly talking divorce? Nobody in the family knows if the marriage will last another day. And the fights are intense. This child takes the worry of what his world could become out into the world with him and is never free to just be a kid.

Perhaps you come from a broken home. What did it do to you when your mom and dad fought? Did you go into your room, pull the covers over your head, and cry yourself to sleep, praying that Mommy and Daddy would continue to love each other? Were you confused, upset, worried, and depressed, wondering what you did to cause this? What happened to your entire world? It flipped upside down. You couldn't be secure in the world because your world had no security. You couldn't be you because you made no sense. The insecurity of your parents' marriage brought pain into your world.

Now let's consider exactly what an unhealthy marriage does to your children's world.

Probably the most important need of your children is the need to know that you and your wife love each other. In fact, I'd be willing to bet that your children would give everything—all of their toys, everything—just to have Mom and Dad stop fighting. I actually counseled a young adult once who said that he would have even given up the love his parents had for him if it meant that they would love one another.

So you see, having parents who love each other is one of the most important needs your children have. Why is it that important? It brings a level of security to the home that a child needs to function confidently and securely in a very uncertain world.

You can certainly see the importance of working things out with your wife. We need to do whatever it takes to make the marriage work well.

Make Your Marriage a Decision

Many people have said that life is about making right decisions. But I believe that even more importantly, it is about making decisions right.

Maybe it doesn't seem now like you made the right decision in marrying the woman you married but where life takes you from here is about making that decision right. See, you can spend the time working on the marriage, reading books, getting tapes, going to marriage seminars, growing, and changing. You can spend the time investing in making your marriage amazing—and in time, it will be—or you can spend the time trying to fix the results of what a divorce brings into your life. One way or the other, I guarantee you will spend the time.

My own parents didn't have the perfect marriage. They fought a lot when I was growing up. They were two different people forced to live one life, as with any married couple. That "loving feeling" wasn't always there. But to them, divorce was never an option. So I didn't go through all the junk some of my friends went through—all the fear and worry. Instead, my parents got all the books and tapes on marriage they could find and went to all the seminars they could. They both worked hard at loving each other. And today, thirty-five years later, they are best friends who are able to enjoy

Having parents who love each other is one of the most important needs your children have.

their family together and to look back at the huge mountain called marriage that they climbed together.

I don't think most men really think about what waits for them on the road of divorce. They don't think through what it will be like to have their children call another man "Dad." What will it be like if the new father has different attitudes and views about raising their children? What if the mom and new dad decide to move to another state? Then these men would only see their kids in the summers and on certain holidays. Another man would do their job of fathering and have their time with those kids—time they could never get back. It's like I heard one little girl say when her parents got divorced: "I went from saying good night to my dad at night to saying good-bye."

If the decision to marry your spouse doesn't now seem like the right one, think about what it would be like to spend half of your holidays away from your children. You'd go from tucking them into bed every night to seeing them every other weekend. You might no longer be a part of their world; instead you might get to peek into their world every so often. Imagine how hard it would be to start a new family while supporting your old family. And what the state would tell you to pay seems like a lot, but in reality, it wouldn't even be enough.

And what would it be like when your kids say, "Dad, please stay here tonight—please stay home."

You'd have to explain to them that their home isn't Daddy's home anymore. With tears in their eyes, they might ask, "But, Daddy, who will protect us, who will watch over the house, who will be there if we get scared at night?" Explain to them then why Daddy doesn't love Mommy anymore.

If at all possible, wouldn't it be better to make that decision right that you made during your marriage vows—the decision to love your wife "till death do us part"?

Let Love Take the Lead

The bottom line is that to be a great dad, you have to love your children's mom. It is your responsibility to love her. Even if she doesn't love you, don't worry about her. You worry about what you can change—and that's you.

My dad said something to me when I was fifteen years old, and it stuck with me. He said, "Son, life is about giving what you have so you can receive what you desire." Did you get that?

You see, if I desire love, I must give what I have, which is love. And when I give it, I open the way to receive what I desire. The problem most of us have is, we are trying to get love. But when you try to get it, you never receive it. When you give it, then it comes back to you.

Maybe you're saying, "But, Scot, she doesn't love me." Try for just thirty days to love her unconditionally. Throughout the day think only about the good things she does, give into her, do what this chapter talks about. In just thirty days you will see her start to love you back!

Your Choices Produce Results

Understand this: Results never precede choice—choices produce results. For example, if I want a raise at my work, I don't get the raise and then work hard. I have to choose to work hard, and that choice will produce a raise. Likewise, I could have the attitude that when my wife loves me, I will love her. No, I must love her first, and that choice will produce the result of her loving me.

Do you want a great wife? It is so simple. Do what my father did: Love the wife you have. "Yeah, but she does this and that," you may protest. No, love her, not for what she does or doesn't do, but because she is your wife.

Think back to the beginning of your relationship when you were in love. What made it different? Your choices. You chose to look beyond the bad, to look beyond what she did or didn't do for you. You chose to bring her flowers, to take her out, to treat her like a queen. When you were dating, you weren't so concerned with meeting your own needs. It was her needs that mattered. You worked hard to win her heart, and you acted as if you were the man of her dreams, which made you the man she wanted to spend her life with. You felt alive and so in love. You felt loved in return, so much so that you promised to spend your life with her. Why? Because you loved first.

But after the wedding, you stopped looking at your wife's needs, and you started focusing on your own needs again. You worked hard for your own heart instead of for hers. Now you don't feel in love with her anymore. You need to go back to the point at which you felt love. Do what you did then, and I promise you, you will feel love again.

So picture this with me: I come home from work one day, and, boy, am I mad. "Holly, I have had it!" I shout. "I have had it up to here with my insensitive actions toward you! I do not communicate or spend enough time with you! This watching sports all the time is getting old. I want you to know that if things don't change, if I don't start loving you like I should, I'm out of here! And if I leave the toilet seat up one more time…" (This represents a typical fight that we all have had, right?)

What's wrong with this picture? In this scenario, I'm upset because I'm not meeting my wife's needs. But in real life, we are usually not upset over failing to fulfill

~

Results never precede choice— choices produce results.

~

our obligations. Rather, we are usually busy worrying about our wives keeping up their end of the bargain.

Think about it. Have you ever had a fight that was not about your wife meeting your need? Have you ever been mad because you were not meeting her need? I can almost guarantee that every single time you have ever been mad at someone, it is because your needs were not being met.

Think about a world in which people worry about others' needs and not their own. Imagine a marriage in which two people are more concerned about the other's welfare than they are about their own. If you will apply this to your marriage, you will have the best marriage since Adam and Eve. Why? Because once you eliminate self, you can put your spouse in her rightful place. What would there be to fight about? "I don't care what you say, Honey, I'm a slob, and it ticks me off. I'm too angry at myself to talk right now…" You see, once you eliminate selfishness, love steps in.

Teaching Love by Example

And do you know what else? By loving your wife unconditionally, you are also teaching your children what love really is and what should be expected in a loving relationship. You are explaining what love in action really is. How your kids love others when they grow up will in large part be determined by how you loved their mother. For example, your sons learn how to treat their wives from how you treated their mother. Your daughters learn what to expect from their husbands from the expectations and standards you set for them based on how you treated their mother.

Many women find themselves in abusive relationships, unwilling to leave. Why? Because they don't know there is anything different. This is how Dad treated Mom, so this is how my husband should treat me, they think. You can see that for many little girls, life with father is a dress rehearsal for love and marriage (I read that somewhere).

Children's ability to trust Dad to lead the family will be confirmed by the things he is doing with Mom. If there is no security in Mom and Dad's relationship, trust will be replaced with fear.

Understand this: Your children need to see you lay down your life for their mother. They need to know you will give it all up for her, that she is the most important person in your life. You treating Mom like that solidifies a need children have inside, and when this need is met, trust is built. It's as if they're saying, "If I can trust you with my mother, I know I can trust you with my heart."

The funny thing is, this goes against what kids actually say. "Dad, come play with us," they whine. "Dad,

why are you going out just with Mom? Take us with you!
Why can't we all be together?" On the "outside" they are
saying one thing, but on the inside dwells a need for Dad
to make Mom number one. There is a bit of security that
is placed in your children's hearts when they see Dad treat
Mom like she is the most important person in his life.

Being a great dad starts and finishes with being a
great husband and loving your wife (or ex-wife). Making
your wife your first priority gives your children a deep
sense of security and trust from which they can go confidently into the world. And although love is a choice, the
results experienced by your wife, your children—your
whole family—will be tremendous.

CHAPTER 5

SEVEN WAYS TO PUT YOUR WIFE IN HER PLACE

My wife, whom I love, has relatives in Ohio—aunts, uncles, cousins, and second cousins. You can hardly go anywhere in their town without meeting someone in the family tree. I want to share a story about a visit we made out there eight years ago.

In Ohio lived little Joshie, a second cousin by marriage, an actual blood relative of my beautiful wife, whom I love. Little Joshie at the time was three years old.

Now let me start with a disclaimer so that I can keep the peace between all those in Ohio and myself. Joshie is now eleven, a straight-A student, and an awesome young man. But on that fateful visit eight years ago, Joshie was different. In just a short time, he actually had me convinced that he was the antichrist. I spent many nights trying to prove to Holly that he was Beelzebub and the end times were drawing near. My scriptures to prove as much were powerful but left my wife still unbelieving.

Joshie and I spent seven full days and nights in what some would call a battle. And all I can say is, I emerged. Not victorious, by any means, but not altogether conquered, either. I just emerged. I emerged from battle with little Joshie ("escaped" might be a more accurate description) and lived to tell about it.

On Night One, the Joshinator, as I liked to call him, during dinner, threw a freshly buttered roll and hit me right in the head. It was a totally unprovoked attack. As I wiped the butter off my face, I could hear that evil, sinister laugh that still haunts my dreams today.

Every morning, little Joshie made sure Holly and I were up at five o'clock. He would bang on the door, give his signature laugh, and run. Any time Joshie had the chance, he would hit me with a blunt object. Out of nowhere, he would walk by and hit me in the shin, the knee, the head, and twice in a more sensitive area. Every toy Joshzilla owned became some sort of weapon used to wear me down. Even in the vehicle, I was not safe from evil. Toys could be secretly launched from any part of the van, fooling all those around us, as they'd say, "Oh, Joshie dropped his toy again."

No, Joshie didn't drop the toy; he threw a weapon and hit me in the head. "Oh, Joshie is so cute," everyone would say. But Joshie was not cute—he was the tormentor!

As this week drew on, I found myself taking great pleasure in tripping little Joshie as he ran by me. I would laugh so hard as he ran away, crying, to go tell. I would think, You can't tell on me; nobody would believe I could do such a thing. No way—it was an accident. No one is going to buy your story. I also found myself asking God how something so wrong could feel so right.

I found great joy in taking little Joshie's favorite toys and hiding them. Holly would open our suitcase and find them shoved in every crack and crevice. She seemed genuinely surprised at first: "Why is Jumbo Man in our suitcase?" she said one day. Excitedly, I said, "Sshhh! He'll never find it in there! Do you hear him crying right now? I think he has noticed it missing!"

She replied, "Grow up."

I said, "HIM FIRST!"

One night, I took Joshie's favorite little blanket, the one he could not sleep without, and hid it under my pillow. I lay in bed listening to him cry, and I laughed myself to sleep. I now understand that if Jesus had come back during that week, I would not have gone in the Rapture. It would have been just me and that little "antichrist" battling throughout the entire Tribulation.

On Day Five of battle, we all went to Holly's aunt and uncle's house. To fully grasp the humiliation I would suffer there at Joshie's hands, you have to picture Holly's aunt. She is the sweetest, most loveable person on the planet. The only person I can possibly compare her with to give you a true picture is Aunt Bee from Mayberry because Holly's aunt wore a little apron

Any time Joshie had the chance, he would hit me with a blunt object.

and was always smiling and baking something. "Scot, do you want a cookie? Some cake? A piece of pie?" You spend two minutes with this woman and your soul craves a hug from her.

Aunt Bee's husband, Uncle Sherb, is by all accounts Andy Griffith. You could just sit and listen to his stories for hours, or listen to him play the guitar out on the porch. I was in Mayberry that day, the greatest place on earth.

So here we are at Aunt Bee's house, and Joshie and I are battling. A "trip" here—a toy jabbed in my back there. Finally, I came to a point where I needed a break. Under our own Geneva Convention, I felt we had an agreement that there was a place of refuge I could go—a free place, a happy place—where no battle was allowed. And I understood this place to be the bathroom.

So off I head to the bathroom and, once inside, I turn to lock the door. But there was no lock on the bathroom door. I don't know why there was no lock (actually, I do know—it's because God has a sense of humor), but with the door decisively closed, I sat down. There I was, sitting down in my most vulnerable position (that's enough information for now).

Think of this from an attacker's position. If you were going to attack me, now would be the prime time to finish me off. This, I believe, crossed Joshie's mind.

So there I was sitting, enjoying the peace and quiet of Mayberryville, when, all of sudden, I heard little footsteps coming down the hall.

Fear gripped my heart. It was just like in the movies when a killer animal is approaching to finish the people off and they're hiding, hoping that if they're quiet enough, the predator will leave. But the animal never leaves, as you well know, because it smells fear. And so did little Joshie.

He walks up to the bathroom. I could see his little shadow blocking the light from under the door. I sensed impending doom lurking on the other side of my dubious defense—an unlocked door.

Joshie pauses. My heart seems to stop. I can hear my own breathing, though I try to hold my breath. Finally, he begins to walk again. Relieved, my heart starts up, and I exhale a sigh of relief. It's quiet for a few seconds when, all of a sudden, just like in the movies—boom!—the door swings open wide. And there stands Joshie in the doorway, buck-naked.

I could tell by the expression on Joshie's face that in his three short years on the face of the planet, he had never encountered somebody being on "his" potty when he had to go. I mean, it had never happened. By the look on his face, I could tell that he was very surprised. I, on the other hand, was very scared.

We stared at each other for what seemed an eternity. I wouldn't blink because I remembered reading that if you stared an animal down, it would not attack. I just stared at Joshie, and he stared back, until, finally, he said (and he said it nicely), "Get off my potty."

With trembling, I said to Joshie, "I swear to you, I am getting off your potty. Please close the door, and in two seconds, I'll get off your potty."

To this, Joshie said with a little more authority in his voice: "Get off my potty."

Pleading, I said, "Please, Joshie. Please. You can go in just two seconds—one, two. I promise I'm going to get off your potty."

Then Joshie screamed. "GET OFF MY POTTY!"

That angered me because I knew he was going to attack. I was at the end of my leash. I thought, You wanna do battle, Joshie? Then let's do this! So with as firm a voice as I could muster, I said, "Joshie, if you don't get out of here, I'm gonna 'bring it,' Boy! And you don't want none of this! So get out of here now!"

In hindsight, that was the wrong thing to say. Joshie let out a spine-chilling battle cry and screamed again, "GET OFF MY POTTY!" Then he charged me like an angry rhino.

There I was, sitting down with my pants wrapped around my ankles—in as vulnerable a position as you can imagine—and I've got this angry naked three year-old running at me. I began to seek God. "God, please help me. I need a miracle, an angel, something—anything. I'm not asking You to part the Red Sea. I'm not asking You for a mighty miracle. Just stop the charging naked boy, please! Get him out of here!"

I continued frantically: "Lord, give me something. Give me a scripture. The Word is supposed to be for every occasion. Give me a verse, some advice, some instruction—something!" And I do believe I heard Him in an audible voice say, "Turn the other cheek." (God does have a sense of humor.)

So here comes Joshie, and he hits me with all of his force, nearly knocking me off the toilet. I regain my balance. He then tries to push me off, all the while screaming, "Get off my potty! Get off my potty!" Still frantic, I say, "Please, Joshie! Please stop!"

Finally, the only responsible thing I could do was to grab Joshie by the face and push him against the bathroom wall. This I did, and he fell down, flailing about. But he hopped back up and charged me again. So I pushed him harder, and this time when he hit the wall, a picture fell to the floor and shattered. Then I just started grabbing stuff and throwing it at him. I threw Kleenex boxes, toilet paper rolls—whatever I could find—but he just kept charging. I was trying to get my pants untangled

Finally, the only responsible thing I could do was to grab Joshie by the face and push him against the bathroom wall.

and up, but Joshie was grabbing my legs and my pants, pulling and pushing in a blind rage.

Now, who do you think is the last person in the world that I wanted to see me half-naked? You guessed it—Aunt Bee. But here she comes, running. "What's going on?" she cries and then screams, "O my God!" Right behind her comes Holly along with several aunts and uncles. Every relative had a free ticket to the "Scottie Show." I wanted to holler, "Why don't you just bring dinner in here!"

Finally, someone was brave enough to come in and grab little Joshie by the ankles. It seemed that it took more than one of them to drag him out as he was kicking and screaming, "My potty, my potty!"

All said and done—our peace treaty destroyed—I retreated to "potty" at the Circle K for the next two days.

Strangely enough, this chapter is about loving your wife. (And I do love my wife. I show her my love and how important she is to me by continuing to go to Ohio to visit her family.) In the rest of the chapter, I will cover seven ways to show your children that Mom is important. We've already established the importance of loving Mom. In this chapter, we will discover how.

In essence, there are seven ways to build trust in your children's hearts through loving their mom. Again, if you're a single dad, do not dismiss this chapter as if it

isn't for you. You need to be practicing these same principles for the mother of your children. Remember, your
children learn the very meaning of love from the example
set by their father.

Number One: Give Her Your Best Time

The number one way to show your kids your love
for their mom is to give her the best part of your time.
Mom has to get the top priority in your attention and your
energy, and particularly your time.

When you get home, the first fifteen minutes of
your time belong to her. Take a time of sharing your day
and talk about what is going on in your life and hers. It is
the best part of your time, and your children need to see
it given to Mom. The kids will likely say, "C'mon, Dad,
play with us! Talk to Mom later." But, no, Mom is to
be so important to Dad that he wants to spend some time
with her first and then spend some time with the kids.

I know you probably want to play with the kids
first and then talk to Mom. But it is important that Mom
comes first. The kids may outwardly show signs that they
don't like it but inwardly it confirms what they need—it
establishes that sense of security in knowing Mom is first
in Dad's life. If you wait until the kids are in bed to give
time to her, the kids don't get to visualize the importance
Mom is to Dad. Do not underestimate the power of such

a little thing! It's just fifteen minutes, but each of those minutes is building trust in the heart of your children.

Number Two: Meet Her Needs

The second thing in the "how" of loving Mom is to make sure her needs are realized. I know we have to buy our kids stuff and we want to buy them the world. But too often we forget what our wives need because we are only conscious of what our children need.

Now, I know all too well how important a woman's needs are, but my biggest question is, why do they have to be such a secret? For men to figure them out is like going on an Easter egg hunt! Women's needs have no consistency, nor do they follow any logical pattern at all. There are times when I'm thinking, Does she need me to talk to her or buy her something? Should I be cleaning something or rubbing her back? Am I supposed to do something with the kids, fix something, open something, close something, say something, say nothing, say more, go here, go there, do this, or do that?

"For the love of God," I plead with her, "tell me what you want!"

She says, "If I have to tell you, it means you don't really care."

Not true, I want to shout, but if you tell me what it is, there is a seventy-five percent better chance that I might actually do it!

DAD

It's time that we as husbands stand up and say to our wives, "What are your needs?" We want to know them so we can meet them. Women know our needs, because our needs are very simple. They do not change like the tides. Food, sleep and sex. If Holly wants to meet my needs, she grabs some chips, takes me back to the bedroom, and then lets me take a nap. There is no guessing here. She doesn't have to sit around trying to figure out what I want. I want food, sleep, or sex—or for a treat, all three combined.

It's important that you don't forget to meet the needs of your wife. Realize that she needs new clothes, makeup and times of pampering. She needs to feel special and important. And she needs presents!

At Christmastime, some moms and dads will decide to buy presents just for the kids. Let me just say that moms are the greatest, because they have no problem giving up everything for the kids. That just proves how much more they deserve gifts. And it is Dad's job to make sure she gets them. I know that to a man's mind, it makes sense to spend that money on the kids, but in the kids' hearts, they need Mom to be treated like a queen. She comes first, and you should spend at least as much on Mom as you do on each child. Why? So the kids can see what she means to you. Kids don't always understand what they hear; they are sight-oriented. Dad says he

> In the kids' hearts, they need Mom to be treated like a queen.

loves her, but what does he get her for Christmas, Mother's Day and her birthday? Does he ever just surprise her with gifts?

"What if I don't have the money?" you ask. Get a second job. That is what my dad did. Scrimp and save all year if you have to. If you put away $3 a week, in one year you could buy a really nice gift. Skip three Big Gulps a week or one fast food lunch every other week, and you now have the money to show your kids what Mom means to you.

It is also your job to make sure your children realize the needs of Mom. It is your responsibility to teach your children to love her and to treat her like a queen. Kids are naturally selfish and self-motivated, and they need to be trained to love. You should be asking them, "What are you getting Mom?" And then you should be telling them, "Okay, you have the best mom in the world; she lays down her life for you. So you can do better than that. Mother's Day is coming up, and we need to make it special."

There's nothing wrong with telling your kids on the weekends, "Let your mom sleep in. Let's do the dishes and clean the house for her. Let's take her breakfast in bed to thank her for all that she does and for being the best. Kids, today is all about Mom."

My dad always made my brother and me buy our mom a gift. We would sometimes protest, "Dad, you can't make us buy her a gift!" He'd just give us the "look," and we'd say, "All right, what do you think she wants?" I remember one year for Christmas, I spent $200 on a necklace for my girlfriend and was planning on spending only $25 on my mom. Dad told me, "Once you're married to a woman, that's fine, but you will not spend more on your girlfriend than on the most important woman in your life. You will spend equal or more on the most important woman in your life now." I didn't have the money to buy two expensive gifts, so Mom got the $200 necklace I bought, and the girlfriend got a $50 necklace!

When you're teaching your kids to meet Mom's needs, make a time of it. I take all four of our kids to the mall and let them pick something out and buy it with their own money. They go from store to store, looking for the perfect gift for their queen. Sure, it takes about two hours, but what it puts in them will last a lifetime. I believe a lot of kids grew up in good homes but were never taught how to love or to give back. So from the teenage years on, they never gave back to the family. Though the family gave their all to them, Dad never trained them to give back.

Last Mother's Day, Baylor had it in his heart to buy his mom this camel he'd seen, a medium-sized stuffed animal. It was by all accounts the ugliest thing I'd ever seen (sorry, Baylor, for writing this but by the time

you're old enough to read it, I am sure you will agree).
This camel actually wasn't just ugly; it was quite honestly
scary. In fact, we later named it "Scary Camel."

But it was Baylor's own money, so I let him buy
Scary Camel for Mom's special day. When Holly opened
his gift, she actually jumped slightly at the sight of Scary
Camel. But to see Baylor's face—that he was so proud
of the gift he'd bought—filled my heart with joy. Baylor
said excitedly, "Mom, you can put him right here (on our
kitchen table) so everyone can see him." That's what we
needed—a demon-possessed camel in our kitchen. Holly
quickly answered, "I think Mom wants the camel upstairs
near her so I can enjoy looking at it."

What makes this story so fun, but, I guess, sad in
some ways, is Holly and I started playing a game called
"Hide Scary Camel." I think I started it by putting the
camel in her makeup cabinet so that when she opened
it up, Scary Camel popped out at her. I later found it in
my underwear drawer, and I returned the favor by stuff-
ing it into her purse.

After that, I was getting my license and registration
out of my glove box for Mr. Officer, and, to both of our
surprise, out falls Scary Camel. Holly was getting some
ice cream, and Scary Camel, cold and frozen, was wedged
into the empty ice-cream container. Then she lifted the lid
of the toilet to find Scary Camel staring angrily up at her.

One of my favorites was when I went up into our attic, and there on the ledge, in the dark, was Scary Camel glaring at me! In the course of one week, I don't know if we have ever had more fun with any single thing. One of us has hidden Scary Camel somewhere but can't remember where. I look forward to the day when one of us gets surprised and gets that great big Scary Camel laugh. Thank you, Baylor, for bringing so much joy to the family with your gift.

Esteeming Mom with gift-giving and teaching your children to love her and meet her needs is your job. This goes for single dads too. Make sure that your kids are loving Mom when you're not around. You should still take them out for holidays to get Mom a gift. You may say, "But she is a total witch toward me!" So what? If you want your kids to live a long life, it starts by honoring Mom. If you want your kids to learn to love back, it starts with you teaching them to give. If you want your children to trust you, it starts by loving the mother of your children.

Make sure they know that divorce is never an option.

Number Three: Never Let Divorce Be an Option

The third thing you can do to show your kids that you love their mother is to make sure they know that divorce is never an option. It is simply never even discussed or brought up. Once it becomes an option, it is only a matter of time before it becomes a reality. Threats of divorce bring only insecurity to your children and to the relationship. And what we're trying to build is security and trust.

Conflict is a normal part of relationships. You get two people in a house together, and you will have conflict at some time or another! As I said, my parents fought when I was young. They even threw Bibles and other stuff! But we as children knew that divorce was not an option. No matter what happened, we knew they would work it out. So their fights never made us feel insecure.

Let's be honest—we never want to fight in front of our children. But I know for myself that, in reality, I will say something stupid sometime this year, and Holly and I will probably fight. We try not to do it in front of the kids, but we know they are okay if it happens from time to time. Actually, if we are able to work through disagreements and conflict the right way, our kids can learn how to work through disagreements and conflict in their own lives.

Holly and I fight once in a while. I call it "sharpening iron" when we do. I read a great book once that said, "As iron sharpens iron, so a man sharpens the countenance of his friend." You can't sharpen iron without having a whole bunch of sparks!

So once in a while Holly and I will have this iron-sharpening ceremony. And we have some interesting ones. But by far, my favorite fights have happened during her third trimester of pregnancy. You see, she's not all there during this time, and I don't mean that in a bad way. But she has a baby growing inside her, and with everything going on in there, I don't think the blood makes it all the way up to the brain.

What makes these fights so amazing is that right in the middle of them, all of a sudden, she gets so mad that she begins to threaten me with what I wanted in the first place:

White T-Shirts and Skinny Sex

Let me give you a couple of examples. My expectations for laundry are very low. It is not my wife's gift and laundry is not her calling in life. So I have very low expectations when it comes to laundry. I generally take most of my laundry out and have it cleaned. All I ask for is clean underwear and white t-shirts. Now, you might be thinking, Just do your own. But that's the funny thing because she gets mad if I do my own! Apparently, the only way she is happy is if no one does my laundry.

Now, the underwear is not that important to me because I can get five days out of one pair. I can turn them around, inside out, upside down, etc. During the great laundry strike of 2000, I made a rainbow with every color but blue. (That is a joke. Please laugh.)

But my white t-shirts—I love them and I have to have a clean white one every morning. For the first five years of marriage, I kept running out of t-shirts. So one day, in my frustration, I went out to the store and bought myself enough white t-shirts so I that would never run out again. I bought forty-five white t-shirts. Mathematically speaking, how often would my wife have to wash t-shirts? I mean, God flooded the entire earth in forty days, right? If she would only do laundry once every flood cycle, I would never run out.

So here it is, Day 46 since I bought the shirts. Who would have guessed it, but I ran out of clean t-shirts. It was early in the morning before work, and I was mad! But I'm smart enough to know that you don't tell a lady in her ninth month of pregnancy any of your complaints. However, I'm not smart enough to know not to talk to myself out loud. (It actually bugs me that I can't talk to myself without her listening!)

As I was walking out of our bedroom talking to myself, I said, "You know, God forbid that I have a clean white t-shirt in the house." Holly shot out of bed like there was fire in it. She then began to let me know all of my faults. Now I only brought up one of her faults (and even then, I did it privately), so you'd think she'd tell me only one of mine, maybe two—I will usually take a two-for-one deal.

That's not how it works. I tell her one, and she tells me all. And as I understand it, I have a lot of faults. In fact, all the problems in the world were my fault at that moment. She blamed me for high interest rates, increased unemployment—she even tried to pin the Kennedy assassination on me.

So five minutes later, we were up to the letter "G" on my alphabetical list of faults, and I was getting even madder. So I burst out, "All I want is clean shirts! You're home all day long. Throw a load of laundry in the wash before your nap. Maybe get up at ten instead of noon and put a load in!" For some reason, this made her madder—go figure.

In fact, she got so mad her eyes turned black, her hair seemed to disappear into her skull, and she began shaking. I knew that whatever she said next was going to hurt. And I admit, I was scared.

Holly just sat there for like a minute. I felt like I was watching a bomb, just waiting for it to blow. Then she said, "I am so sick and tired of your whining and complaining! I swear to you—I promise you—you will never run out of white t-shirts again! I'm going to wash them day and night. You're going to have white t-shirts up to your eyeballs! YOU WILL NEVER RUN OUT OF WHITE T-SHIRTS AGAIN!"

I felt like I was watching a bomb, just waiting for it to blow.

I'm thinking, sarcastically, Please don't give me lots and lots of clean t-shirts. But the way she said it made me so mad. For whatever reason, I yelled back, "The heck you will! Don't you go telling me that I'm going to have a lot of clean t-shirts." I walked away thinking, There! I told her!

It wasn't but a few days later that it was sharpening time again. This time, Holly made me so mad, I pulled out the secret weapon—the sex card. As I said, this is a weapon men reach for anytime they're in a fight and it looks like they might lose. They don't play that card often, but the funny thing is, when they do, they bring on a bigger fight. (I mean, it will be big!)

Realize that at the time all this "sharpening" was going on, Holly was nine months pregnant (I think she gave birth five days later). I hadn't seen any "action" in a long time, and it was affecting me. I was having blackouts and I seemed to sweat all the time. My hair was falling out. I was seeing Scary Camel in my dreams, and Scary Camel was always wearing some Victoria's Secret© Lingerie. I'm just no good without sex.

When I played the sex card, it looked like Holly's eyes were going to roll back in her head—scary! But, again, she just sat there. Then she began slowly, with deliberate fury, "When I have this baby and lose all this weight, I'm going to be skinny, and you're going to be having skinny sex all the time. You're going to have it in the morning, at lunchtime, dinnertime, bedtime, in the middle of the night... You will be having so much skinny sex, you won't be able to walk!" She screamed, "YOU'RE GOING TO HAVE IT UNTIL YOU BEG ME TO QUIT!"

Again, I'm thinking, Please don't give me lots and lots of skinny sex! The way she said it made me mad, and for whatever reason, I responded, "The heck you will! Don't you go telling me that I'm going to have a lot of skinny sex!" I walked away thinking, I told her!

There is an old proverb that says "iron sharpens iron." You hit two pieces of iron together, and you will get some sparks. Holly and I sharpen the daylights out of each other. But it's all part of growing, changing, maturing, and learning how to act in the relationship until the day comes when the husband and wife are two sharp pieces of iron who rarely need any re-sharpening.

Normal fighting doesn't bring insecurity, but talking about divorce and leaving do. Choose today never to use those words, never to speak them. Don't even talk about taking a break from each other; no, you need to sharpen each other. I read a really good book once that said "do not let the sun go down on your wrath." When you and your wife experience conflict, you make sure you work it out before you go to bed.

All it takes is one time for you to say divorce is an option, and, just then, a seed of insecurity gets planted in the hearts of your children. Now, if you have already done this, you sit down as a family, apologize and affirm to one another that divorce is never an option.

Number Four: Go on Dates!

The fourth thing you can do to show your kids that Mom is the love of your life is to take her out at least every other week. I believe in going out every week if possible and taking at least one trip a year, just the two of you. If your relationship is important and the heart of the family, treat it like it is. You need to make time alone together a priority, and it is your job, not your wife's, to do it.

Sure, it is easier if your wife plans it and makes all the arrangements. However, if you plan it, you will be surprised at the results it produces in your marriage. If you take the initiative and spend ten minutes planning a date, it says so much to your wife about the importance you place on time spent with her.

Also, let your kids know that Dad is taking Mom out. Our kids usually object: "Daddy, take us too!" I tell them, "I love you so much that I won't take you." They don't understand that, but my point is, I love them so much that sometimes it's just about me and Mom spending time together.

Don't get all caught up with the idea of everything being about the whole family. When the kids move out, it will still be just you two. If you don't build a relationship, or if it is built around the kids, one day it will fail. And a divorce when your kids are adults is equally as hard on them.

"Well, Scot," you may argue, "money is tight, and we're too busy to go out just the two of us." Money was tight for my parents; my dad worked ninety plus hours a week just to make ends meet. My parents were busy too. But somehow my dad also made time to run a youth group, and my mom made time to run a children's ministry. And Dad would take Mom out and they'd split a plate at a cheap restaurant. They'd have a date, whether it was just talking, walking in the park, or riding bikes. They found some money and made the time.

So stop the dumb excuses. I think I've heard them all. Why put off building trust in your children? You probably had less money when you met her than you do now, but you found a way to go out on dates.

"But, Scot, baby-sitting is expensive!" Then find another couple to trade baby-sitting trips. You watch their kids one week, and they watch yours the next. Get rid of cable TV, high-speed Internet, fast food, sodas, and that gas station cup of coffee every day. That's enough money right there to take her out for a nice date every

If your relationship is important and the heart of the family, treat it like it is.

week. A great relationship with your wife will bring much more joy to your life than cable TV and a Big Mac. It is your job to find a way to take your wife out on dates!

Number Five: Voice Your Commitment

A fifth important way to love your wife is to voice your commitment to her. It is very important for your children to hear you say how much you love their mother and what a great wife you think she is. Confirm what they know in their hearts—that you are blessed to have her.

Tell your children your dating stories and share all the good times you had and are having with the woman of your dreams. Make sure they hear how much Dad loves the most important person in their lives, their mom.

When your children are older, think about renewing your wedding vows. Let them be a part of the ceremony so they can hear the commitment you make to each other all over again.

If you're a single dad, tell your kids how blessed they are to have their mom. Tell them what a great person she is. Teach them always to see the good in her. Never talk badly about her and never put her down. If you do, with every negative word about their mom, you chip a little bit of trust away from your own relationship with your kids.

Number Six: Show Her Affection

The sixth way to show your kids how much you love their mom is to show her affection in front of them. I'm not saying to make out like my sex-starved parents (that would do some damage), but you do need to show some affection.

Voicing your commitment to her is one thing but demonstrating it is another. Your children want to see you kiss. Your older kids may say, "Get a room!" but inside, it is confirming what they want to know—that Dad cares. They like to see their parents hug and hold hands in public. But make sure you're not just doing these things for outside show; do them all the time.

Number Seven: Agree With Her

The seventh best way to love your wife and build trust with your kids is to agree with your spouse. In other words, back her up. Kids will play you and your wife against each other if they can. They'll ask Mom first for something they want. If they get the wrong answer, then they'll ask Dad. One of the greatest things you can give to your children is agreement with your wife. When you and your wife are in disagreement, the kids in a sense, win because they get what they want. But they actually lose because they don't get what they need.

When my kids ask for something, I'll say, "What did Mom say? If you asked Mom, don't ask me." I back her up. And if you don't agree with one of your wife's decisions on something, never say it in front of the children. Back her up in front of them and then talk privately. Then you can make it look as if she changed her mind. But never undermine her authority. It is your job to strengthen her authority, not weaken it, in the eyes of your children.

Your mindset should be to make your wife look good. Your mindset should be: I will stand up for her. Maybe it doesn't make me look like the nice parent to my kids, but it shows that I esteem their mother. In doing so, it strengthens my place as a father.

Now I didn't learn this lesson all at once. It took a couple of times of doing it the wrong way. I'll give you one instance that will explain what I mean.

So here I am alone with the kids. Mom is out of town. Holly leaves me with two rules: One, the kids go to school, and two, they don't play with match-es. I feel that, as a thirty-year-old man, I can handle both of these.

Problem is, I'm not good without my wife—it really is true. When I have no reason to go to bed, I don't go to bed. I stay up and play video games all night long. But then at seven o'clock in the morning, when Laken comes in to get me up for school (it is sad when the five-year-old is the responsible party), he says, "Dad, can I stay home from school today?"

In my mind, a battle begins. I hear one side of my brain say, We need to take Laken to school, while the other side (my favorite side) says, We need sleep!

No, Laken needs to be taken to school—that is what a good dad would do, my good side argues. But the other side replies, How can we be a good dad if we're tired? We need sleep to be at our best.

That is an amazing point, I think to myself. Then my better half of reasoning chimes in, No, the child must learn today.

Wait! Says my favorite side, What if we do school at home today! Being at home can be an even better learning experience. We will work on reading, writing, and math today at home.

Yes! I think. This is a revelation from God. We will do school at home, and school will begin at noon. But wait—with every good plan, evil will try to destroy it. What if Holly finds out? She would never understand a word from God like this.

So I finally say to Laken, "Do you want to do school at home with Dad today?"

He says, "Yes."

I say, "Okay, but don't tell Mom."

> Your mindset should be to make your wife look good.

So Laken and I have a magical day of fun and learning. It turns out to be all that God planned it to be. We do biology by playing at the park. We do oceanography by playing "Jaws" in the pool. We study nutrition while eating a Happy Meal. And we study the justice system in America while watching *Judge Judy*. We wrap up the school day by studying current events while watching the news, and we end with learning finance while playing a game of kids' Monopoly.

That night, Holly calls. The first thing she says to me isn't, "I love and miss you," or "You're the greatest husband in the world." No, it's this: "Did Laken go to school today?"

How dare she even insinuate such a thing to me! I say, "Honey, it hurts that you don't trust me."

She repeats, "Did you take Laken to school?"

Without lying, I say, "Yes, Laken had school today!" (That, my friend, is no lie; it is deception, which in some religions is a very acceptable practice.) We then talk for a while, and she says, "Let me say hi to Laken."

I hand Laken the phone. And what do you think is the first question out of this untrusting woman's mouth? That's right—she asks him, "How was school today?"

I want to scream at her, "How can we have a marriage if you don't trust me?" And then I listen as my son, who just moments earlier was my best friend and closest companion, says, "School…uh…school…uh-hum…" He then looks over to me for something. I'm frantically motioning, Just hang up, Son! Just hang up the phone! I'm trying to get the phone, while Laken is still mumbling, "School…we did uh…"

As I try to yank the cord out of the wall, this child, who all day had been singing praises to Dad, suddenly turns on me and says, "Mom, Dad made me stay home from school! I wanted to go to school, but Dad wouldn't take me! (Long pause.) Okay, Mom, love you," and then hands me the phone: "Here, Dad, the phone's for you."

That was the last time I ever did something like that.

As dads, we are to back Mom up. We are to build her up and take her side. In this, we build trust in our relationship with her and in our relationship with our kids.

Growing up, my father expected, or actually demanded, that more respect be given to Mom than to him. We could mouth off a little and get away with a little more with Dad, but we had to be very careful about what we said or did to Mom. He esteemed her needs higher than his own and he backed her up all the way. Basically, the unspoken rule in our home was, if you hurt Mom, be very afraid.

Mom's value in the home needs to be esteemed. So protect and uplift her needs above your own. If you don't, when the kids are teenagers, Mom will become a nuisance—a pest—to them, and they will have no respect for her. It is sad that in today's society, we have boys cursing at their moms and girls slapping their moms. Why? Because Dad didn't esteem Mom.

To this day, I have a healthy sense of fear about respecting my mother. When I was about nineteen years old, I was still living at home while going to college. One of my responsibilities was to feed my dog. But Mom's responsibility was to buy the dog food when she went shopping. Well, we ran out. I was having kind of a bad day, and my mom said something that just struck me wrong. She said, "Why didn't you feed the dog today? Go feed him right now!"

I responded, "If you would get off your rear and buy some dog food, I would feed the dog." Now, I have no idea where that came from because I never talked to my mother like that. But all of a sudden, my dad jumped out of his chair and walked me up against the wall. He whispered in my ear like Dirty Harry, "Don't you ever talk to my wife that way again!"

To this day, I have never talked that way to my mom again.

In my father's house, you just didn't come against his wife, his love. You didn't hurt the queen of his house. We as dads have to stop wanting to be the "good guy" to our children and stand up and be the man we should be in the home. This has to be our attitude.

I love it when Holly and I wrestle, and my boys take Mom's side. I want that. I want my kids in the middle of a fight to say, "Dad, be nice to Mom! You're playing too rough." I want my kids to stick up for their mom. That way, when they are teenagers, I will never have to be concerned about how they treat the most important woman in my life. Also, in setting this bound-ary, I am showing my children that they can trust me with their hearts, just like Mom can trust me with hers.

I hope you can see that these seven ways of lov-ing your wife are the building blocks of establishing trust in your home—trust that begins in your marriage and that translates into confidence and security for your entire family.

To this day, I have a healthy sense of fear about respecting my mother.

CHAPTER 6

LIVING A LIFE OF NO REGRETS

Here we are on our family vacation to San Diego. My parents have rented us the beach house of the year. This house has all the amenities of the rich: computer light switches, a 20'-by-20' sliding door that opens the house to the beach, plasma TVs, a home movie theatre, a swimming-pool sized bathtub that you can do laps in, and so forth.

So here I am bringing all forty-three bags in from the van to the house. On about trip thirty-seven, Baylor, my four-year-old at the time, says, "Dad, you just have to see the sink in the bathroom! It's just my size!" I think to myself, That's kind of cool as I continue my back-breaking getting-settled-in routine. Baylor continues, "Come and see it, Dad!"

"Let Dad finish bringing in the luggage first," I reply. "I only have about seventeen more trips." Baylor insists, "But, Dad, I can sit on the toilet and wash my hands at the same time!" I walk away amazed at Baylor's favorite beach house amenity while in the back of my mind wondering, Why is the sink so low and so close to the toilet?

Finally, I bring in the last bag, the scrap-o-rama bag. I throw it (because no one is looking) against the wall. Just then, Baylor cries out, "Come and see the sink, Dad!" I have never seen my son so excited about anything, so I head upstairs and turn the corner just in time to see Baylor sitting on the toilet and washing his hands in a bidet. He exclaims, "Dad! You can even get a drink out of it…"

I scream, "Baylor, NO-O-O-O-O!"

If you boil life down to what really matters, you will find that what matters most will be that thing that you want most to have at the end of your life. No man on his deathbed ever said, "I wish I had spent more time at the office. I wish I had spent more time with my business associates. I wish I had watched one more *Survivor* episode. I wish I had a couple more useless baseball statistics clouding my mind."

No, most men who are honest will say, "I wish I had spent more time with my family. I wish I had invested more into my children. I wish I had different memories of my time with my family. I would give anything to spend one more day at Disneyland watching my children's faces light up, to watch them one more time running through the waves in the ocean."

Listen closely, friend: Life is about creating memories.

DAD

I want to have great memories of what I've done with my family. You see, when the kids move out and go live their own life, what I have left of their childhood is the memories of times spent with them. When you look at life like that, it changes how you approach every single day. You'll get up with the thought, How can I make a memory today with my family? or, What type of memory will I be making today?

You'll get home from work and figure out what kind of memory you can make with your kids that night. Do you make the memory of Dad sitting in front of the TV—which could be just one great block of memory that will stick with them—or do you make a memory that brings a smile to their faces, a memory of time Dad invested in them?

Realize that what you do with your children, the memories you build with them, will carry on for generations to come. I pass stories down to my children of the priceless memories I have of times spent with my dad. What's amazing is that we often don't realize how the smallest of gestures, the simplest of times, can create a lifetime memory.

For example, I can remember almost every Tuesday night "family night" we ever had, laughing and doing crazy things like changing the game Monopoly to "Cheatopoly"—a game in which the goal was to cheat (this

> Listen closely, friend: Life is about creating memories.

was not a character-building game!). I can remember every single vacation we ever took—from the simple camping trips when Dad pitched our tent on a hill to the Disneyland trip when he had us staying in the $9-a-night hotel (in an area of town where we saw prostitutes walking the street outside our window).

I remember the trip to the Grand Canyon. We drove five hours to get there, got out of the car and looked at the big hole. We said, "Cool!" got back in the car, drove to the hotel, and stayed there for the rest of the week.

I remember the times of hunting, fishing, and the trips to Grandma's house. I remember the birthday parties, the awesome Christmases, and all the other holidays. My mind is full of all the great memories we had while growing up. There are so many good ones that they overshadow the bad. In fact, I can't even remember very many negative things that happened during my growing-up years.

Dads are the ones responsible for creating memories. It's not Mom's job, it's not the kids' job—it's yours. You see, if you create memories and invest time when your kids are young, when they get older, they will still want to create memories with you as well as create memories with their family when they have one. The father who sits around complaining about how his kids never visit him doesn't realize that it is his own fault. If he didn't sow any great memories into his family, it will be impossible to reap any great memories as a harvest.

The world operates under the principle of sowing and reaping. If you sow time into your kids when they're young, you will reap time with them when they're older.

It is true that when your children are younger, it's hard to play games with them, because, to be honest, those games aren't much fun for us adults. There are many things we would rather be doing than that. But then when our children are teenagers and can play all the really fun games, in their mind, there are a lot of other things they would rather be doing than spending time with their parents! But if Dad created a habit in them, as we saw in Chapter One, he sowed time into them when they were young. And now the kids are sowing back into him.

Do you remember that Harry Chapin song "Cat's in the Cradle?" That song, in a nutshell, perfectly captures the sowing-reaping cycle of parenting.

A child arrived just the other day.
He came to the world in the usual way.
But there were planes to catch and bills to pay.
He learned to walk while I was away.
And he was talking 'fore I knew it, and as he
grew,

He'd say, "I'm gonna be like you, Dad.
You know I'm gonna be like you."

And the cat's in the cradle and the silver
        spoon,
Little Boy Blue and the Man in the Moon.
"When ya' comin' home, Dad?" "I don't
        know when.
But we'll get together then.
You know we'll have a good time then."

My son turned ten just the other day,
Said, "Thanks for the ball, Dad. C'mon let's
        play.
Can you teach me to throw?" I said, "Not
        today.
I got a lot to do." He said, "That's okay."
He walked away, but his smile never dimmed.
He said, "I'm gonna be like him, yeah.
You know, I'm gonna be like him."

Well, he came from college just the other day
So much like a man, I just had to say,
"Son, I'm proud of you. Can you sit for a
        while?"
He shook his head, and he said with a smile,

DAD

"What I'd really like, Dad, is to borrow the
car keys.
See you later—can I have them please?"
I've long since retired. My son's moved away,
I called him up just the other day.
I said, "I'd like to see you if you don't mind."
He said, "I'd love to, Dad, if I could find the
time.
You see, my new job's a hassle and the kids
have the flu,
But it's sure nice talking to you, Dad.
It's been sure nice talking to you."
And as I hung up the phone, it occurred to me,
He'd grown up just like me.
My boy was just like me.[1]

He regrets the time he missed out on because he was too busy to invest time in his son.

Now, what is that song about? Regret! It is about a man who today regrets the relationship he has with his son. He regrets the time he missed out on because he was too busy to invest time in his son. He regrets not having good memories in life.

This chapter is about you living a life of no regret.

I was reading an article a few years back about regret. In it was a survey of men between the ages thirty-five and sixty-five. More than eighty percent of them had a considerable amount of regret in their lives. In men over the age of sixty-five, more than ninety percent of those men had a considerable amount of regret.

I imagine that they regretted their relationship, or lack of one, with their wives or they regretted the way their children turned out. Maybe they regretted not having much of a relationship, or many memories, with their children.

Once parents' kids are out of the house, a father may be left having nothing: no memories of family times together, no memories of vacations together. Sure, at that time in their lives, he saved a few thousand dollars, but maybe he blew that money on gadgets and stuff that are all broken now. Had he invested that same money into the family, he would have had thousands of price-less memories to treasure once the children were gone. Sure, that father saved a few hours a week by not having a regular family night. But maybe he wasted that time on television shows that today he can't even recall. Sure, he can tell you almost every baseball statistic since the game's inception, but he can't tell you the hopes and dreams inside the hearts of his children.

Wasted time spent away from the family, doing things that later mean nothing, is a major problem in America today. I don't want to live a life of regrets. I don't want to be one of those Americans who possesses nothing more than memories of time wasted on myself and on what I considered to be the pleasures of life. I want to be 110 years old, living a life of no regrets, looking at my wife's hot body (sure she'll be 110, too, but she'll have the body of a ninety-year-old woman!), and knowing that I spent wisely the time given to me on the earth. Holly will still be my best friend. I know one of us will have to die first, but I hope it will be me, because I can't imagine one minute without her. Holly and I have millions of memories of time spent together because I make sure we go out on a date every single week. I make sure we take a couple of mini vacations, just the two of us, every year. I make sure that when I get home from work each day, she gets the first part of my night, talking and sharing about life.

When I'm 110, I will also be thinking about the relationship I had and continue to have with my kids, who also are my best friends. I'll remember the thousands of hours of great memories together, the thousands of hours of family nights we had every week and the great vacations we took together every year. And because I'm investing in them when they're young, they will continue to invest in me when I'm old. My kids will come visit me every week, not because they have to, but because they want to. They will honor me, not because the Bible tells them to, but because they love me and desire to spend time with me.

Learn To Value Things Appropriately

That will be my life. What about yours? The secret to having this kind of life—a life of no regrets—is to learn to value and esteem things appropriately.

I'm sure we've all watched *The Price Is Right*, the TV game show hosted by Bob Barker. Whether you know it or not, you can learn a lot from Bob Barker. This is what I call "the Bob Barker Principle of Life." On the show, what happens when you over-value an item? You lose it! You lose that item, and everything else you've earned, too, even if you over-value it by just one dollar.

The same goes for life. When you over-value an item, you risk losing it, and you can also lose all the things you undervalue. Everything in life has value. If you want to live a life of no regrets, you have to learn to value things correctly.

The guy who values watching sports may actually over-value sports. Now sports have value; I enjoy watching them from time to time (okay, a lot of the time). But if you find yourself spending a few moments with the kids on the weekends and then watching eight hours of football, you have over-valued football and undervalued time with your kids. And one day when the kids are out of the house or don't want to hang out with Dad because they now have things more valuable than him, he will have regrets.

Get this. If you value time with your kids when they're young, they will value time with you when you're old. But if you value time with other things when they're young, they will value time with other things when you grow old.

You see, under the Bob Barker Principle of Life (let's call it the BBPL), you find the time, money, and resources for those things that are valuable to you. Similarly, you will find excuses not to do those things that are less valuable.

Let me give you an example: One day I was on the golf course counseling a guy about his marriage. I talked to him about the importance of date nights and spending time with his wife. He responded with, "Right now, money is a little tight for date night. And time—I just don't have the time!"

I thought to myself, You just told me about the last six golf games you played each Friday. You were able to plan ahead, call and make a tee time, but you're not able to plan a "wife time." Give up a couple of hours each week and spend time with your wife. And you also spent sixty dollars today to play with me. You have two thousand dollars worth of clubs. Sell them and work on your marriage if that's what you have to do!

At the end of your life, when you can't pick up a golf club anyway, who cares about the 300-yard

~

The guy who values watching sports may actually over-value sports.

~

drive? When you have no relationship with your wife, who cares about keeping up your game? Would you be willing to give up one of the greatest things in life—a best friend, a companion, someone to share life with—for golf?

You see, golf to that man I counseled was more valuable than his relationship with his wife. Because it was more valuable, he was able to find the time, money, and resources to do it. Now golf has value. Go out and play if you like. Just remember that golf is not more valuable than your relationship with your family; if it is, you risk losing that thing you undervalued—your own family.

If you don't learn to get your values in order, you will find yourself with regrets in the years to come.

It isn't just what you say that counts, either. Because I know we all say, "Hey, my family is important, and my wife is important." Don't look at what you say; look at what you do. That will tell you whether you're headed toward regrets in life.

You might say your family is valuable, but what you might do is spend a few minutes a night with your children and then watch two hours of television. Now, watching TV has some value to it. It's relaxing. But is it more valuable than your relationship with your family? If it is, you will end up with regrets in life. You'll end up wishing you had done things differently where your wife and kids were concerned.

No one on his deathbed says, "I wish I would have seen one more episode of *Seinfeld*." But he might say that he wishes he could hold his kids one more time, spend just one more day at Disneyland, or spend one more day at the beach with his family.

You might say your wife is valuable, but what you might do is tell her, "Sorry, Honey. I don't have any money to buy you an outfit or to take you out this week. I just don't have the time to sit down and talk to you." Yet you don't blink an eye at the $100 cable bill so you can get 7,000 channels! You're unbothered by the $300-a-month Harley motorcycle payment so you can be cool. (Really, I would rather be a great husband and father than be "cool.") You found time to watch all 200 hours of the NBA playoffs, but you had no time for your wife.

Owning a Harley may have value. Cable TV has some value. But when they are more valuable than your wife, you will end up with regrets.

You might say, "Sorry, Honey, I don't have time to take a parenting class or go to the marriage seminar" (the class is one whole hour a week). Yet you have time to watch a three-hour football game, hit a bucket of balls twice a week, and read the sports page so you know what is going on in José Conseco's life. You can take golf lessons so you can learn to direct a stupid ball into a hole. But you can't take parenting lessons so you can learn to direct your children toward success or even to find out what is going on in their lives. You take golf lessons to fix your newly discovered slice, but you don't have time to take a marriage lesson to fix your marriage that has been broken for five years.

You need to examine your own life. This may be your value system but as soon as you revalue your life, it will change where you spend your time, money, and resources.

Do you want to find out what is really valuable to you? This week, go through your checkbook and find out where you're spending your money. Then go through your schedule and find out where you're spending your time.

Let's look at a sample checkbook for a month's time and see where this husband and father is headed, either to a life of regrets or no regrets.

- $800 for car payments
- $100 for 7,000 channels of cable
- $100 for high-speed Internet
- $300 for motorcycle payment
- $200 for golf green fees

- $100 for payment on golf clubs
- $50 for the kids to go to Chuck E. Cheese
    pizza
- $40 to take wife to dinner

Let's also look at a sample schedule for the week:

- 12 hours watching NCAA tournament
- 10 hours watching miscellaneous TV (two
    hours a night)
- 6 hours watching movies
- 3 hours at the driving range
- 4 hours golfing
- 2 hours washing cars and motorcycle
- 2 hours doing yard work
- 2 hours wandering around the garage acting
    like he's working
- 3 hours taking naps
- 3.67 hours with kids (20 minutes a night and
    two hours on weekends)
- 1.5 hour date with wife
- 4 hours listening to wife talk while wonder-
    ing when she will stop so he can watch TV
- 7 hours listening to music or sports on radio
    while driving
- 0 hours listening to self-improvement tapes

As soon as you revalue your life, it will change where you spend your time, money, and resources.

- 0 hours reading self-improvement books
- 3 hours reading newspaper
- 7 minutes reading Bible
- 20 minutes (exaggerated) of prayer
- 6 hours at the lake
- 1.5 hours of church (attending three times a month)

Is this life headed for regret? This person almost spends more time reading the newspaper than with his wife or kids. He definitely spends more time golfing than with wife and kids. He wastes nearly one day per week on things that will in no way ever better his life, and he spends no time on things that will make his life better—like reading books and listening to self-improvement tapes. At the end of life, what good did those thousands of hours of easy-listening radio or sports-section stats do him? They left him only regret.

Now I'm not saying you can't listen to the radio, read the paper, or play golf. They have value, and we need to relax and enjoy life. But if those activities are over-valued, you will end up with regrets in your life.

Have I made my point clearly enough? Determine to live a life of no regrets!

---

[1]Chapin, Harry. Lyrics by Sandra Chapin. "Cat's in the Cradle." Verities & Balderdash. Electra, 1990.

CHAPTER 7

CREATING MEMORIES

It is a warm spring day as the family takes a drive to Grandma and Grandpa's house. Off in the distance is a huge hot-air balloon taking off. It's exciting to see your children enjoying things for the first time. I look into the rearview mirror to see Laken, now three, light up with excitement and surprise. For the past few months, Laken has been impressing us with his new-found ability to put sentences together. Out of nowhere, my child—who has been brought up in a Christian home where we have spent our lives pouring God's Word into him, instilling character into his little soul, and trying to train him up in the way that he should go—says in a slow, dramatic voice, "W..H..A..T IN T..H..E HELL IS T..H..A..T!"

I think that maybe I heard wrong, so I ask, "Laken, what did you say?"

He then says it a little slower so I can understand him: "What-in-the-hell-is-that!"

I look over at my wife and say, "Where in the hell did he learn to talk like that?"

Some of my low-life habits that I am breaking still leak their way into my children once in awhile.

In order to live a life of no regrets, we must get our values in order. Right values will mean we live a life of no regrets.

First make sure that people are valuable to you. Of course, your wife and kids will be the most valuable to you.

You know your values are messed up if you "lose it" on the freeway when someone bumps your car, because that inanimate object—your automobile—is more valuable to you than people. You have to wonder about your value system if you allow your kids to talk back to your wife and treat her like garbage—but heaven forbid if someone loses the remote control! When your kids backtalk their mom, you're cool and disinterested, but when your prized television equipment is not readily at hand, you're ablaze with passion, ready to discipline all those involved!

One way to start getting your values in order is to take on the responsibility of creating memories in the home. I will suggest some practical things you can do. Let's start with the bare minimum. We covered some of this in the last chapter, but I want to encourage you again. Starting this week, figure out what night is going to be family night.

Growing up in our house, Tuesday night was family night, and my dad made sure nothing—I mean, no emergency, no friends, no relatives—ever messed with our family night! As a kid, that made me feel that family time was important to Dad. We meant more to him than anybody or anything. It created a sense of unity and an attitude of togetherness. Once a week, we knew for sure we were going to work on our relationship as a family—only, it wasn't work; it was great fun.

And you know what? Family night doesn't mean we went out to a restaurant or spent a lot of money. We didn't have a lot of money growing up, so family night usually consisted of playing a game together. We played all kinds of games: Uno, Scrabble, Monopoly (or "Che-atopoly"), Life, Family Feud, Trivial Pursuit, War (the never-ending game), Mille Bornes, Nertz (our family favorite), Hearts, Crazy Eights, Old Maid, Go Fish, 500, Spades, Rook, Hangman, marbles, memory games, charades, and so forth.

Some nights we would build card houses or even put together LEGOS® and Lincoln Logs. We would build paper airplanes, fly kites, make ice cream, fon-due, and ice cream floats. We would watch movies, ride bikes, picnic at the park and barbeque, swim, go to drive-in movies (these are better than regular movies, because you get to have more talking and relationship time), go fishing, have water-gun and balloon fights, play hide-and-seek and tag.

> You have to wonder about your value system if you allow your kids to talk back to your wife.

We would put together puzzles, build models, and build rockets and watch them blow up while never leaving the ground. (One time we had a "spend-two-hours-trying-to-start-the-gas-toy-airplane-that-never-started-while-dad-said-bad-words-under-his-breath" night.) We had BB gun-shooting night, slingshot night, build-a-fort night, and a catch-bugs night. We made wooden racing cars, baked cookies, baked bread…and so goes the list. Are you getting some ideas now?

I have so many vivid memories of our family nights, it's scary. And now this is what I want my children to have. Like me, I want them to be able to fill up a book with memories of "family night." (Even as I write this, I can't help but smile as memories pass through my thoughts. I can't help but say what a great childhood I had thanks to my mom and dad making family night a priority in our week.)

So schedule it! Don't just say, "This week, we will have family night some night." It won't happen until you schedule it for a particular night. And you will not believe how excited your children will get about this. When Baylor was just three years old, he had no clue about the days of the week or of time in general but come Wednesday morning, he knew: "Dad, family night is tonight, right?"

Schedule it and then fight for it. Make sure, if at all possible, that nothing gets in the way of family night.

Another practical thing you can do to change your values and create memories in the home is to plan the family vacation. Now this is something you have to plan, schedule and make sure happens every single year. Sometimes it may sometimes be tempting to think money is too tight but you could use that same excuse every year until the kids are grown and out of the house.

Vacations are times when you get away from all the problems and stresses of life for a minimum of five days and focus primarily on each other, on relationships, and on memories. You can't put a price tag on that. What's amazing is that you can do this for a very reasonable amount of money.

As I said, we had very little money growing up, but Dad made sure we had a vacation every year. Maybe it was going to the Grand Canyon and staying in a cheap hotel. Sometimes it was camping, like the time Dad borrowed all the equipment, took us out in the woods, and almost starved us to death because he didn't pack enough food. Then there was our trip to Disneyland in the $9-a-night "hotel" that I already told you about. We had a ski vacation and a beach vacation, both while staying in cheap hotels.

Our vacations growing up were never about the money spent or even about the places, but it was always about the relationships. Our dad made sure we had a vacation every single year. He put away $10 a week (that was one fast-food trip we didn't take, videos we didn't rent, or popcorn we skipped at the movies). At the end of the year, we had about $500 for a vacation.

If you make it a priority, you will find the money.

Maybe you're thinking to yourself, We will just vacation at home and spend time together there. But you won't. You'll do housework, call friends and deal with all the everyday demands of life. No, you have to get away from everything and focus on each other to create a warm, lasting memory in the hearts of your children.

A week away is the minimum requirement to build those strong family memories, but I suggest you also do at least two mini vacations a year. Try to take a couple of days every year camping, skiing, or boating. You have Spring Break and Winter Break—use these times wisely. Be creative and remember that the most important thing you can do is make memories for your kids. When your kids are out of school, your attitude has to be, What can I do with this time to produce a great family memory?

On that same note, we have to get the mindset that weekends belong to the kids. That is another time to create a memory. I realize we have work to do on the house and "honey-do" lists to accomplish. But try getting those things out of the way first as a family and then spend a few hours together. My family gets up on Saturday mornings, eats breakfast together, and then we all clean the house and work in the yard together as a family.

I realize that this won't be one of your kids' most fun memories, but it puts in their hearts the importance of unity and of giving back to the family. The reward is that you then get to do something together, whether it's a picnic, a swim day, or a pizza night.

Of course, when your kids get older, you have soccer games, baseball games, football games to attend—you name it. But it's important that even at these games, you go together and participate as a family. The idea is that you go watch and support your brother, and he will do the same for you. We always make it fun and exciting with snacks and treats.

What was hard for me to adjust to was that before I had kids, Sundays for me were church and sports day. I love—and I mean love—football! When football season is over, a part of me seems to die inside, and that part doesn't come alive again until the next season in September. For me, trading football time for time playing t-ball in the backyard was hard at first, especially since I work for a church. I don't get home from church until about 1:00 p.m., and I have to be back at 4:00 p.m. to preach.

But I refuse to lose a whole afternoon to something as meaningless as football (it hurt me to write that!).

Before I had kids, Sundays for me were church and sports day.

Now I tape the games and watch them Sunday night after the kids are in bed. Sunday afternoon is all about them. And you know what? I found that when I used to have that Sunday nap, I was actually more tired at church that night than when I forced myself to go out and play with the kids. After a couple of hours outside, I was energized to go preach!

You see, I know the time will come when the kids are grown up and out of the house. I hope and pray that because I gave my Sundays up for them, they will still spend Sundays with me, coming over with my grandchildren and having "Dad" time.

Think about it—what could possibly be better than spending time with your kids? Friends come and go, but family is forever. Sure, we need time with friends and even getaways with friends. But that time should never replace the time we spend with our kids. I know I fight hard to make sure that every week we get as much time as possible creating memories together.

Next on the list for creating memories is to make sure that holidays are special. Never let a holiday go by without celebrating it together. A great holiday celebration creates powerful memories for your children. There are so many great things you can teach your children concerning giving, particularly during the Christmas season—how good it feels when you give, why we give, and how to receive. Be sure to make Christmas special. Get the tree together if you pick out a live one each year, plan a night for family decorating, put up lights on the house, or plan a night to go out looking at lights. Make that time of year special for the family.

While we're talking about Christmas, let me remind you that presents are never an option; you should always get them for the family. "Well, this year we're just going to give to the poor," you tell your family. But come on! You will have the poor with you always, and your family is your priority. Now I'm not saying that we shouldn't do something special for the needy. In our family, we take our kids out and have them pick out a special toy for an unfortunate child and help pay for it out of their own money. It is important to teach them to give outside of the family, but we should never sacrifice giving to the family in order to do it. If you do, there is a good chance your children will grow up resenting giving to the poor.

In our family, we make sure that each child has something special under the tree. (And of course, I make sure my wife has something from me that says, "Mom is the best, and this is to say thank you for all you do.") Now, your kids' presents don't have to be expensive gifts; it's not about money, but about sacrifice and thought.

I received a garbage can, of all things, one Christmas when I was a child! It was a Green Bay Packers garbage can to be exact. And while it may sound stupid or cheap, I know my dad had to put away some extra money for that. But he knew how much I loved Green Bay. It came nowhere near the cost of my friend's $300 bike, but I guarantee it meant more to me than his gift did to him. It would have been easy for my dad to say, "We have no money for gifts this year." And because I love him, I would have happily said, "Okay, Dad." But my dad bought an amazing memory for just $12.

The gift doesn't have to be great, but it does have to be special and maybe even involve sacrifice of some sort.

To me, Christmas was an amazing time of family, of giving and of receiving. It was a whole month of anticipation and love. Christmas is about memories, thanks to parents who never let one go by without making a special time of it.

Birthdays are the same way. I have heard families say, "Let's not make a big to-do about birthdays." Why not? It gives you an excuse to create a memory and to celebrate the day that God brought your child into your lives. A child's birthday is an awesome day and deserves to be celebrated. Make your kids feel like this is a huge day, and make them feel important—like life would not be the same had they not entered your family. Once again, you don't have to give them expensive gifts, but they do need gifts. They need a cake and a day of celebration, of laughing and of being together with their family.

Of course, you need to make sure all the siblings buy something for the birthday boy or girl, too. Teach them the importance of giving to their siblings. Put that habit in their hearts, and it will continue the rest of their lives.

For the rest of the holidays, get on board with Mom. Do the Easter egg hunt. (As a grown-up, I actually did the egg hunt with my parents until I had kids myself. I was twenty-four years old, hunting for eggs at my parent's house! And even then, my parents made it fun with riddles and clues they had spent hours writing.) Plan the Memorial Day barbeque, the Fourth of July fireworks, the Labor Day trips. Change your attitude to seeing these days as opportunities to create memories with your family.

As your kids get older, allow them to help out with the planning of family night, holidays, and vacations. When they get to help in the planning, they are more excited about the doing.

Finally, plan to have a "date" at regular intervals with each child. I have four children, so I do something

> ∼
> Christmas is about memories, thanks to parents who never let one go by without making a special time of it.
> ∼

special with one of them each week. Our date isn't hours long. It may be just going and getting a Slushy or a Happy Meal. It may be taking a walk or taking them along golfing and letting them steer the cart. I feel it is important to have that one-on-one time with each of your children when you really talk to him or her. Having a special outing with a child helps him open up and talk about the stuff in his life and about what is going on with him. Then when he does, you can really listen to him as you let him talk.

This is especially valuable concerning daughters. They learn how to date and what to expect from men by watching you. If you fill that father-daughter need, she is less likely to go off looking for it later in another man's arms. I suggest you also encourage your wife to take the boys out for the same reason. Boys learn how to treat women properly from times like these spent with Mom. They learn how easy it is to talk to a girl, and it helps them overcome that fear of the opposite sex.

As your children get older, let them play a part in planning some of the family nights. Let them be a part of planning the vacation activities. When you involve them, it makes them feel included. And when you're a part of the vision, it makes you more excited to help create the best memories possible.

Also, I encourage you to get a family hobby. It might be camping, water skiing, snow biking, bike riding, hiking—the list of possibilities could go on and on. But whatever you choose, make it a family hobby that you can all do together. We recently bought "quads," or four-wheelers, and we take them up to the mountains once a month. It's something fun and different that we can all participate in together. Our city kids get a chance to go out into the woods and ride their quads, build forts, shoot BB guns, build campfires, and so forth. It gives us an excuse to get together. I spent $10,000 on these quads, so I guarantee we will ride them this month! Our hobby, in a way, makes us make time for family, fun, and memories.

Please do what I've talked about in this chapter: Create memories with your children when they are young, and then you will experience what my parents have today—kids who still spend all their holidays with them and who still take one vacation a year together.

Maybe you don't have a lot of special memories of time spent with your own dad. Yes, your dad was a provider, and he protected you. He was there. But memories were never built. A relationship was never developed. I want to challenge you to break that cycle. That cycle of lack of relationship can end with you.

Look for memory-making opportunities, and, instead, in the final analysis, you will end your life with a big smile on your face. As your life flashes before your eyes, it will be filled with priceless images of time spent with your family.

If you're looking for great ideas to create memories of your own with fun family nights, creative vacation ideas or to post ideas of your own, go to:

www.DadMomBook.com.

CHAPTER 8

LIAR LIAR!

At the time this story took place, my son Laken was six years old. One night after being tucked into bed, he was somehow able to wiggle out a loose tooth, his second tooth to lose.

Laken comes out of his room to notify Dad, who has just purchased the "Madden 2000" football video game and is switching gears from great dad to All-Pro Linebacker for the Green Bay Packers. It's 8:05 p.m., and my child's needs are playing a close second to sacking Peyton Manning. So when Laken says, "Dad, my tooth came out," I didn't catch my cue that the Tooth Fairy had some responsibilities that night. When Holly went off to bed and reminded me to make sure the Tooth Fairy took care of his responsibilities, it just didn't register. I had bigger things in mind to take care of, like converting on fourth and two!

To properly set this story up, let me give you a brief background. My younger son, Heath, had $2 that he kept in a basket by his bed. The day before, my youngest son at the time, Baylor, had gotten into the basket and had taken Heath's $2. My wife found him with the money, didn't know where he'd gotten it, and put it in a drawer. This is annoying information, perhaps, but it is very important.

Dad the Super Bowl champ finally goes to bed. The next morning Heath wakes us up by saying, "Dad, Laken won't get out of bed."

In a stupor, I answered, "Let him and Dad sleep." Half an hour later, Heath says, "Dad, Laken is just lying in bed and won't let me turn on the lights."

"Son, just leave him alone," I said. Approximately one hour goes by, and here comes Laken, not just crying but sobbing. It's a cry that tells you your child's innermost being has been hurt. He says, "Dad, Heath turned on the lights, and now the Tooth Fairy won't come."

Suddenly, it clicked. Laken had been lying in bed for the past two hours acting like he was asleep, waiting for the Tooth Fairy. My wife looked at me with eyes that said, "You might just be the worst dad in the world."

So while my wife is telling my son how irresponsible and self-centered the Tooth Fairy is, I run downstairs, open my wallet, and find—nothing! I'm trying to think fast: I could write him a check, but that probably won't fly. I start opening drawers to see if I can find some change. I open one particular drawer and—boom!—it is a miracle orchestrated by God! There lay two one-dollar bills. I grab the money, run upstairs, and shove the money under Laken's pillow. I run back into our bedroom and interrupt the love of my life explaining to Laken how it seems the Tooth Fairy only has time for his own needs and that the needs of others don't matter.

I'm out of breath, but I manage to get out the words, "Son…(gasp)…go check your pillow again. Maybe the Tooth Fairy came." He runs into his room, and I hear him holler, "Dad, the Tooth Fairy came, and she gave me two dollars!"

It was at that moment precisely that Heath hollers, "Hey! Where's the two dollars from my basket!" He continues: "Laken, that's my two dollars! Mom, the Tooth Fairy took my money and gave it to Laken!"

Holly looks at me with a look that says, "How low can you sink, stealing money from your own child?" I'm shaking my head wildly, "No!" as she storms off to the boys' room. I chase after her. As we approach, we hear a scuffle. Heath and Laken are both wrestling and crying. We pull them apart, and Heath screams, "I hate the Tooth Fairy! She's a stupid robber!"

Needless to say, my children to this day don't fully trust the Tooth Fairy. Whenever Laken loses a tooth, Heath makes me help him hide his money.

In case you haven't figured it out, this chapter is about the importance of keeping your word. The fact that I have to write about such a subject annoys me somewhat

~

We pull them apart, and Heath screams, "I hate the Tooth Fairy!"

~

because it is such a foundation to trust. Keeping your word is the key element in building a trusting relationship. How can a child possibly trust a father who doesn't keep his word? How can a child trust the advice of a father who, over the years, has never been consistent with his promises?

Liar, Liar...

A great homework assignment for you would be to watch the movie *Liar, Liar* as a visual illustration of what a father's broken promises can do to the heart of a child. The movie is about a dad who makes promises to his son that he has neither the intention nor ability to keep.

It's a great movie, but isn't it funny how we as adults can watch a movie and forget about any questionable things in it—things that, say, a six year-old shouldn't see? I'm speaking hypothetically, of course. But that brings me to another personal illustration of the detrimental effect a lie can have. This happened on another one of our family vacations.

Holly had gone to the store, leaving me alone with the children. I thought, We could all relax and watch a movie together. But I knew if I watched one more Disney movie, I would snap, since I had listened to "Heigh-ho, heigh-ho, it's off to work we go" for the last eight hours in our automobile. So I looked through our selection of movies and said, "Let's watch *Liar, Liar*." My thoughts were that it's a great character-building movie, and it's clean and has no cussing (or at least not any more than Dad driving for eight hours while listening to seven small, annoying men whistle).

So I put the movie on and cuddled up with my five- and six-year-old sons. Soon, however, I dozed off to sleepy land—you know, that light sleep, in which you are kind of aware of your surroundings but can't really figure out if it is a dream or real.

That's where I was. It was in this dream-like state that I kept hearing something to the effect, "…It's probably because you have big boobs. I want to box them, Ma-ma!"

Over and over, this strange phrase played in my mind, but I also kept hearing small children laughing in the background. Finally, I couldn't take it anymore. I opened my eyes to see my children rewinding the tape back to the beginning of a scene featuring a girl with big "you-know-whats." My sons were watching and laughing so hard, they both kept falling over. I said, "No! We can't watch this!"

Just then, Mom walked in. I quickly turned off the evidence—I mean, the TV. Holly asked pleasantly, "What have you guys been doing?"

I tried to say, "Bible study," but Laken piped up, "We're watching *Liar, Liar!*"

Holly looked at me and asked, "Is that an appropriate movie?" Of course, I responded in the affirmative: "Oh, yeah, it's very clean." But just then, both children began reciting word-for-word that entire two-minute scene, including the part about "boxing them." It was at that point that we (the kids and I) were grounded from watching movies for the remainder of the trip.

My point is this. I don't want to be like the father in that movie, who says things but doesn't follow through. I want my children to realize that when Dad promises something, I will do all I can to make sure it happens. Part of the reason that's so important to me is that when they are in their teen years and I say something that contradicts what their friends are saying, I want them to hold true to my words. In their hearts, they will know Dad has never lied before—that what Dad says always turns out to be true.

To build a trusting relationship, a father must keep his word to his children.

I don't know if you realize it or not, but your children hold on to everything you say. So we'd better be careful with those statements we just throw out there, such as, "Hey, kids, this weekend, let's go to Chuck E. Cheese." Then when the weekend comes and goes, Dad once again filled the child's heart with an empty promise. Or Dad promises that he will be at the child's next soccer game, but then something comes up and Dad can't make it. Sure, he had an excuse. But to have an excuse is to admit you're wrong—that's what my daddy has always said.

Grandpa's Famous Fishing Cabin

Your child makes a mental note of every broken promise. Think back to when you were a kid. You probably have some memory of a parent or an adult who made empty promises. You have memories of promises you held on to and were disappointed.

I know I have those memories. My grandfather, for example, was a great man. He was a great father to my mom, and, in a lot of ways, he was a great grandfather. But aside from the many good things he did as a grandfather, only one thing sticks out in my memory: For the love of all that is good and holy, he never took me to the @!#$%&! fishing cabin!

Let me explain. My earliest memory of Grandpa was when I was about four years old. It was Christmastime, and Grandpa sat me on his knee and told me about this magical place called the "Fishing Cabin." It was a place near a lake so far back in the woods that trucks couldn't get there—a place where fish practically jumped into the boat. Deer came and ate food out of your hand.

To build a trusting relationship, a father must keep his word to his children.

He promised, "When you get older, Grandpa is going to take you to the Cabin." At four years old, my heart skipped a beat. It was the most anticipated event of my life.

Each time Grandpa and I would talk on the phone, he would tell me about how much fun we would have at the Cabin some day. He would tell me about his last trip there and about all the fish they caught. Finally, the summer came when we would go spend time with Grandpa. I was in the seventh grade, and we would be at Grandpa's for three weeks. That whole year, all Grandpa talked to me about was how much fun we would have at the Cabin that year.

When we arrived, the first thing Grandpa said was, "We're going to catch so many fish when we go to the Cabin!" I could barely sleep each night, because tomorrow, I thought, could be the day we would finally go to that magical place in the woods we'd talked about for so many years.

But each day, Grandpa had another reason why that day wouldn't work and why the next day would be the day. Finally, twenty-one days later, as Grandpa was loading us up in the car to go home, he said, "Sorry the fishing trip didn't work out. Grandpa had a lot of things come up but next time, we'll go fishing and we'll catch so many fish..."

As he was hyping it up this time, I remember thinking, But what about yesterday and the day before when you sat outside drinking with your buddies? What about last weekend when you sat inside watching television all day? What about the week before when you worked in your shop, tinkering around for two days? Do you think that because I'm young that I'm not smart, that I don't see or comprehend? At that moment, I thought, I love you, Grandpa, but I don't trust you.

From that moment on, anytime Grandpa made any promise to me—whether it was the fishing trip or just coming out to see us—I remember thinking, Sure, Grandpa, whatever you say. And any time he ever told a story, I remember thinking, I wonder if that really happened?

Even as an adult, I still had conversations with Grandpa about the fishing trip we would take "next year." He was still promising me that twenty-six years after that fact—when I was thirty years old! I would say to my wife, "Why does he still lie to me?"

The last year of his life, he came out to visit us for a month. I honestly remember not trusting anything he said. If he said, "Friday, let's get together and do such-and-such," I would think to myself, Whatever, Grandpa. I'll believe it when I see it. All those years later, I still had a hard time believing anything he said because he had disappointed me so bitterly as a four year-old.

The day of Grandpa's death, I got an e-mail from him, and in the e-mail, he talked about the great fishing trip we would all take together that year at the Cabin. Up to the day he died, he was still promising me that fishing trip!

Now, I do not intend this story to be hurtful to my family in any way. I simply want to show you how a simple promise—just one—can potentially destroy trust in a relationship. Grandpa had good intentions, and I know in my heart he wanted to take me fishing. I know that it was fun to get me excited to see him and to be with him. But the damage of his broken promises outweighed all the positives in my relationship with him.

I know how fun it is sometimes to excite the kids with, "Hey, this summer, let's go camping." And maybe at the moment, you really want and intend to go. But understand that your kids recorded what you said in their memory, and if summer comes and goes and you don't go camping, you just lost a good portion of your credibility with them.

"Well, why wouldn't my kids remind me of something I promised them?" you might ask. The question is, why should they have to? To me, it wasn't my place to say, "Grandpa, take me fishing today." He promised, and since he was the adult, I figured I would wait until the time was right for him. I was sure up to a certain point in time in my life that he would eventually make it happen.

I think the best thing a father can get out of this chapter is to keep his mouth shut when it comes to making promises to your kids unless you are sure you can fulfill the promises you make. If you're not positive you can go camping this summer, don't say anything. Then when the time comes and you can go, it will be a pleasant surprise for the kids. If you're not sure you can go on a picnic this weekend, don't raise false expectations. Wait until Saturday morning, and if it works out, it will be an exciting surprise.

One of the most detrimental things you can do to your children is to build up false expectations. Think about your own life and how mad you get when your expectations aren't met.

For example, let's say that every morning when you go to work, you know and expect that there will be a lot of traffic on the freeway. Although it doesn't make you happy, since you expect it, you don't blow your cork (most of the time). But let's say it is a Saturday at noon. You get on the freeway with the expectation that there will be no traffic. But once on the freeway, it is bumper-to-bumper traffic. How frustrated does this make you? The situation is the same as it is

One of the most detrimental things you can do to your children is to build up false expectations.

every morning on your way to work, but your expectations are different on this particular day.

Look at it this way. Let's say that all day, your wife makes sexy comments about what will happen in bed that night, some of which are illegal in seven states. All day you are so excited, you can barely walk. You can't wait to be alone with her at last. But that night, as you crawl into bed, you notice she is already asleep.

Now you're mad. It's not that you would ordinarily get this mad because you don't necessarily expect anything. But you begin to wonder, Why would she talk that way all day and set me up only to do this? Why would she say it if she wouldn't do it? It would have been better if she had never said a word. Then if things worked out for a great night of sex, it would have been a pleasant, welcomed, surprise for her husband.

You see, your word is so important. It raises people's expectations, and nobody gets their hopes up like children. So if you even think you won't be able to do a certain thing with your children, don't say that you will. If you do promise you'll do something with your children on Saturday, for example, then do everything possible to do something with them on Saturday. Make it happen. And if you tell your children that you're going camping this year, get it on the books and start making plans—barring nothing! Remember, your children don't want your excuses; they want a trusting relationship with their father. They want you to be a man of your word and to back up with action the things that you say.

Your word means everything. In fact, the rest of this book will be worthless if your word is worthless. You will never develop a relationship with your children if they can't trust every word that comes out of your mouth.

Can you trust someone who never keeps his promises? How much faith would you have in a financial advisor who constantly lied to you? Would you give him control of your finances? No! Likewise, do you think your teenager will give you any control in his life if he can't trust what you say? No!

You may think your children are too young to remember your broken promises. But I was only four when Grandpa promised me that infamous fishing trip (which, by the way, did I mention, NEVER HAP-PENED!). I can picture in my mind the conversation like it happened yesterday.

My son Laken was only three years old when I realized that even at his young age, children know when you don't keep your word.

I brought home a video game one night at about his bedtime. So I said, "Tomorrow before bed, we will play this game." The next day I forgot. It was seven o'clock, and it was bedtime. I remember Laken throwing a big fit about going to bed, which was very unusual. Although he didn't like going to bed and whined a little each night, it had been quite some time since he had actually thrown a fit about it. With a forceful voice, I said, "Knock it off and get into bed!"

As I was tucking him in, I could tell he was really troubled by something. After about twenty minutes of my asking what was wrong and his saying nothing, finally as I was leaving the room, he said, "Dad, are you going to play that game after I go to sleep?"

My heart dropped. I said, "No, Son, you and I will go play that game right now."

What if I had dismissed the whole situation as his being rebellious or overly tired or just spoiled and had sent him off to bed? I could have lost a little bit of his heart that night.

Keeping your word has to become a priority in your life. Am I saying you can never break your word? No, of course not. Things do happen. Maybe you had to finish something huge at work, and you missed the soccer game. Or it rained and you couldn't have the picnic you'd planned. But how are you characterized? Do your children trust in the fact that you will do everything possible to keep your word? At the moment of truth, will they think, Dad missed a soccer game. Something big must have happened because I know that my dad does everything in his power to keep his word?

If that is the heart of your children, then if you do have to cancel something that you'd planned together, it doesn't bother them. Why? Because they trust your word.

Keeping your word needs to be a lifestyle. If your kids see you lie or break your promises to others—especially to the most important woman in their lives, their mother—it constantly sticks in the back of their minds, I wonder if he would do that to me. Once again, broken promises bring judgment.

Even more responsibility weighs on single dads. Make sure your kids know you will do everything you can to make sure your visitation happens, that nothing gets in the way of that. Make good on your promise to send child support, and make sure it is always there on time. Make sure if you tell their mother you'll do something, you actually do it. Keeping your word is a key part in developing the relationship with your children that you desire.

If Mom says not to take the kids to see a certain movie, don't say okay and then sneak off and do it and tell your children not to tell her. If you only knew how much damage that does to your relationship with your child and what you are teaching him or her to do as a teenager, it would scare the heck out of you.

Do your children trust in the fact that you will do everything possible to keep your word?

So let your yes be yes and your no be no. Anything more than that carries the potential of ripping away at the core and foundation of your relationships. Remember, building trust is the core of your relationship with your kids, and the key way to do that is to always keep your word to them.

CHAPTER 9

I'M SORRY—WHAT DID YOU SAY?

While driving along one day, Baylor, age four, suddenly asks Holly who the devil is. Holly answers, "Well, he's a bad guy who wants to get you to do bad things. And he wants to try to take your stuff." Baylor thought for a minute and said, "You know what, Mom? I don't think I'm going to hang out with that guy."

I applaud Holly's ability to really listen to our children, and I admire her heartfelt answer to what was a serious question to our son Baylor. And our kids listen to her, too. Baylor seemed to hang on her every word as she explained Satan to him. (I'm going to remind him of what he said if he ever even thinks of hanging out with "the bad guy.")

Just the other night, Holly was going on about how I don't listen to her and—blah, blah, blah—I really wasn't paying attention. Then it came to me: Communication is a vital part of any relationship. While nodding my head and saying, "That's right, Honey" while she went on and on, in my mind I wrote this entire chapter.

Communication isn't always about just what you say; it's also about what you do. It has been said

145

that words only account for ten percent of what we communicate; our body language, tone and actions account for the rest.

Like you, I want to communicate love, security, and trust to the hearts of my children. The right kind of communication is at the heart of trust. It is the "blood" that brings nourishment to the "body," or the relationship (a corny analogy, but nevertheless true). In other words, if communication doesn't exist or isn't good communication, the relationship can't grow and function properly. Many relationships suffer "heart attacks" (if I may continue my corny analogy), and sometimes they're fatal because Dad lacked the skills of communication.

Now, there are different ways of communicating in which we as dads must become developed. For example, there's the "problem-solving" side of dad that says, "Hey, we need to do this and that. Please go do it." Then there's the "discipline" side of dad that says, "Do this and that—or else!" While neither of these ways is wrong, necessarily, they are not the ways of communicating that I'm going to discuss in this chapter.

There is a way of communicating that most dads miss; it is the communication that builds the relationship with their children. It is communication that allows each person to share those deep things inside, such as hopes, dreams, aspirations, and feelings. In this type of communication, we share a part of ourselves—who we really are—with one another.

The reason dads need to learn this type of communication is that we want to communicate love to our children. In communicating love, we provide a safe atmosphere that fosters trust. To communicate love is so much more than just saying the words. I read a great book once that said "…faith without works is dead." In the same sense, words without actions are dead. We have all had relationships with people who've said, "I love you," but nothing in those people's actions lined up with their words.

You may have had a father who said he loved you, but growing up, you felt no love. My goal is for my kids to go out into the world every day and feel sure about their dad's love. I want my actions to line up with my words so that my love for them is never in question. My kids may question the love of those outside the family, but Dad's love is never in question.

Love is an action; it is something you do. So dads, let's do love.

> The right kind of communication is at the heart of trust.

Communicating Love With Actions

You may think your actions agree with the words you're communicating to your children but there's an aspect of putting action to words that I want you to consider. You may think you're loving someone with your actions, but whether you realize it or not, the person could be missing the significance of your actions, because those types of actions do not indicate or express the love they need. We all have what are called love languages, and love languages are how we give and receive love.

(This next section is a brief overview of Gary Chapman's book *The Five Love Languages*.[2] I strongly suggest you read this book. Reading it changed my life.)

Because a particular love language is how we receive love personally or individually, we tend to think everyone else receives love the same way. But in reality, that may not be true. So you may be doing all kinds of things for your wife, for example, and after a while, you starting feeling like, What the heck! She is so unappreciative.

At the same time, she is upset with you because, in her mind, you never show her love! In reality, it's not that you don't love her; it's that you aren't loving her the way she needs to be loved.

Let me give you an example of how this works in the parent-child relationship. A dad comes home and says, "Son, I bought you a wooden glider today. Why don't you go out front and fly it around?" The dad who shows his love for others with gift-giving does so because that's how he best receives love. When someone gives something to him, he feels loved by that particular action. So to show love, he gives gifts. And he feels that his actions are indications of his love.

But suppose this dad's son, on the other hand, likes quality time. Having quality time with someone he loves makes him feel loved by that person. So the gift of the wooden glider doesn't mean as much to him. He would give anything in the world if Dad would take a walk with him and talk with him—or come outside and fly the glider with him!

If Dad doesn't recognize his son's "love language," he will go through life feeling like he gave his son the world but was never appreciated for the love he showed him. And the son will grow up having never felt loved by his dad. Once again, it wasn't that his dad wasn't giving love to his son; it just wasn't the right type of love.

Here's another example. Maybe a dad feels love best through spending quality time together. He says, "Hey, Son, let's go for a walk and get some ice cream." But his son never really wants to go. So the dad feels like his son doesn't want to spend time with him and is rejecting his father's love. In the meantime, the son, who is best loved by acts of service, feels rejected by his father.

This son would love it if Dad would come out and work on his bike with him, help him build a fort, or help the coach of his baseball team. When it doesn't happen, that boy may grow up feeling like Dad wasn't there for him, which is untrue. Dad was there—just not in the way the son needed him to be.

Many fathers are frustrated because their kids act like their dad doesn't love them. If that describes you, it's not necessarily that you're not trying to love your kids, but it's probably true that you're not loving them in the way they need it most. In other words, you're not communicating your love in the most effective way for them.

What good is giving something to someone else if it is something he or she doesn't really need? If we're going to communicate love effectively, we need to find out what our loved ones need and then give it to them. As fathers, we need to learn the languages of love and find out what each of our children's primary love languages are. Then we can make sure we are communicating love to them through those languages—through those ways of communicating love.

The Five Languages of Love

There are five primary love languages, and here is a brief overview. (But, please, get the book. It is more comprehensive, and if you want to be really good at something, you need to fully understand it.)

The Giving of Gifts

Love language number one is what I call the "show-me-the-money" or the gift-giving language. There are those who feel most loved by receiving gifts. These are the people who, when they get a birthday card, first shake the card to see if money drops out. What the card says inside doesn't matter as much as what falls out of it!

Now, to "speak" this language to your kids, you don't have to buy huge, expensive gifts. You could just get them something that says, "Today I thought of you." Right now, in my nine year-old's life, this is his main love language. It's not that all kids don't want gifts, but to some kids, gifts tend to be a little more special. I can come home with gifts for all my kids, but Laken carries his gift around for days. He shows everyone what Dad got him. Heath, my eight year-old, plays with his gift for ten minutes, and then off he goes. He's very thankful for the gift, but the gift itself doesn't communicate love to him like it does to Laken.

> To some kids, gifts tend to be a little more special.

Acts of Service

Love language number two is what I call "What have you done for me lately?" or acts of service. This love language is communicated when you do something unexpected or outside the norm for someone. For example, if I come home and my wife has taken out the garbage for me, that is love communicated by an act of service. (Or maybe she washed some white t-shirts for me!) Because I am an acts-of-service person, that blesses me. She did something for me that she knew I would appreciate, and that makes me feel loved.

For your kids, this particular love language of acts of service may be communicated by fixing their bike, building a tree house, or in their teen years, helping them work on their car. Some of my greatest moments as a teen were the times my dad would spend working on my car with me.

As I said, I am an acts-of-service guy, so this love language comes naturally to me. Some dads may miss it because they're gift-givers, so they'll say, "Hey, Son, I will pay someone to fix that." The dad feels like he's showing love to the son, but if the son's love language is acts of service, the father is missing an opportunity to love his son effectively.

Now, you may not be good with cars or tools, and paying someone is the right route to go. But you must find other ways to do something for your child. It may be coaching his little league team or washing his car for him unexpectedly. (And don't pay someone to wash it. It's a love gift from you, so you do it.) To a gift-giver, that may sound stupid. His attitude is, Why do it when I can pay someone to do it for me? Stupid or not, your acts of service mean more to this child than your gifts.

Quality Time

Love language number three is quality time. Some people love to just sit and talk and share life. Quality time requires that you give yourself to the conversation; you listen closely and give the appropriate responses. Realize that time is a factor in showing love through spending quality time, but you must also realize that you don't need three hours at a time to show love to someone who is best loved by quality time spent together. You may spend only ten or twenty minutes, but to that person, those few minutes made his or her whole day.

A child whose primary love language is quality time needs time each day when Dad listens to him tell about his day. A ten-minute walk, sitting out on the swing or driving to the store may be all you need to do. So if your love language is acts of service and your child's is quality time, you could go out and wash his car if you want. But he or she will think, Thanks, Dad, but I would rather that you just talked to me. I can wash my own car but I can't have a conversation with my dad without you.

Words of Encouragement

Love language number four is words of encouragement. For some kids, you can say, "You are so good at that," and it lights up their countenance, while other kids just say, "I know." If your daughter's "language" is words of encouragement, or affirmation, you could tell her, "That dress really looks amazing on you" and that one little phrase will fill her "love tank" for the whole day.

This love language is simple to communicate. Just look for areas in which to encourage your kids. You don't want to flatter them, but you do want to find sincere ways to say, "You're great at that."

I believe Heath, my eight year-old, is motivated by this love language. When I say, "Son, you are so good at gymnastics! You're a natural," he gets this half smile on his face and gives me an embarrassed little nod. But then he walks away with a skip in his step. On the other hand, I can tell Laken, "You are very good at baseball," and he looks at me and says "I know, Dad."

Showing Affection

The last language of love is physical touch and closeness, or affection. To some people, a big hug, a hand on the shoulder, or an arm around them during a movie fills them right up with love. A person who's motivated by touch also loves just to spend time with someone he loves. What makes this different from quality time is that you don't have to talk to communicate love. You can just be around each other. So you could be cleaning the garage while your son is working on his bike in the garage. You're not having some deep conversation; you're just near each other. This time spent together means the world to this child.

If physical touch and closeness describes your child's love language, plan time when you can just be near him or her and give this child the extra hugs he or she needs.

As you read this, you might be thinking, My kids have all these love languages. They want the gifts, the service, the time, the words, and the touch— they want it all! In some sense, this is true. You have to realize that your kids' true love language won't really emerge until they're about eight years old. Your kids need to be loved in all these ways, but your job as a parent is to find the one or two ways that are especially meaningful to them. So study these languages, knowing that your kids possess a need for each one, but one or two will be the most important to them as they get older.

> To some people, a big hug, a hand on the shoulder, or an arm around them during a movie fills them right up with love.

Conflict Resolution: Understanding Our Differences

After you understand the five languages of love, you can see why so many fights and arguments happen in relationships over the years.

My wife, for example, is a quality time person, with a secondary language of physical touch and closeness. (I was genuinely surprised when I found that physical touch wasn't sex. I wanted to add love language number six—sex—this being all men's primary love language.) My love language is acts of service and gift-giving. (So if Holly buys me something and cleans the house—man, I feel loved!)

Before we read the love language book, a typical night consisted of the following. I would come home from work at least once a week with some sort of gift for her, and she would say, "That's nice. Thank you," and then sort of toss it aside. That annoyed me. She would then follow me throughout the house, talking to me while I cleaned up, put things away, and fixed things—until she would get mad because I wasn't listening to her. At that point, I would get mad because she seemed unappreciative of all the things I was doing for her.

Then on the weekends, Holly would want to do what I thought were some of the dumbest things ever. "Hey," she'd say, "why don't we drive to Payson?" (Payson is a town about a two-hour drive away.) When I would ask why, she'd say, "I don't know. Let's just have lunch up there."

I would, of course, respond, "No, let's just drive right up the street, have lunch, and come home, clean the house, and wash some white t-shirts." You see, Holly wanted that closeness of just sitting and talking in the car all the way. To me, that's my version of what hell would be—just one long drive…

When you understand and begin to communicate these love languages, they will change your life. You'll understand your wife's language, your kids' languages, and maybe even your boss's language. If you learn, for example, that your boss's love language is gift-giving, you could give a little extra gift on Boss's Day or on his or her birthday.

If it's acts of service, you can do things beyond what is expected of you in your job description. You could clean your boss's office, or you could carry his or her things to the car. And if your boss's language is physical touch, you could just hold him or her for long periods of time! Remember, a pat on the backside can sometimes go a long way. (All kidding aside, please leave that physical touch language alone in the workplace!)

What I'm trying to say is, you need to use these love languages to communicate effectively with your kids and with those closest to you. Learn how to nourish those relationships with their life-blood—communication.

Learning to communicate correctly teaches your children the love and security they need to have a healthy, trusting relationship with you. Remember, communication isn't always just about the words you say; it's about your actions, too. When you begin to understand your

children's love languages, then you can truly communicate love to them, which, after all, is the highest goal of
being a great dad!

---

[2]Chapman, Gary, *The Five Love Languages: How to Express Heartfelt Commitment to Your Mate*, Chicago: Northfield Publishing,
1995.

CHAPTER 10

I STILL CAN'T HEAR YOU

One time my son Heath had been complaining for a week about having a stomachache, so, finally, I took him to the doctor.

It's interesting to note the difference in our parenting when we had only one child compared to four. Had it been a few years and three children earlier, with our first child, we would have rushed him to the hospital the first day of the bellyache. When Laken, our firstborn, would get a 101 degree temperature, we would rush him to the nearest urgent care facility at two in the morning. But now when a child comes to me with 104 degree temperature, my attitude is, "Nothing wrong with you boy. Man up. Finish throwing up and go outside and play! HEY, DON'T YOU PASS OUT IN MY HOUSE!!!" With our firstborn, I had gone out and bought a $150 first-aid kit. (I think you could perform a complete triple bypass with that thing!) If he fell and scraped his knee, I was ready to operate.

Once we had a few more kids, my concerns, because of time restrictions, had to change. I don't have the time to rush everyone to the hospital every time something happens. "Who told you that you could cut yourself? Don't you get no blood in my house. Pick that finger of yours off the floor and get outside with yourself."

With our firstborn, I was one of those weird, protective dads. I was so afraid of germs that I boiled everything. In fact, if I was at home, you could guarantee there was water boiling on the stove. If Laken's pacifier fell on the floor—splash—I threw that thing in boiling water for ten minutes. Now with my fourth child, I can find the dog chewing on the pacifier, take it out of the dog's mouth, wipe it on my pants and put it back in Peyton's mouth. "Oops, sorry, Peyton. I got a little dog hair there around your mouth. Let Dad wipe that off for you."

You understand I'm mostly kidding, right? In any case, it took a week of his complaining with a stomachache for me to take Heath, who was three years old at the time, to the doctor's office.

After sitting in the waiting room for a brief two hours and then in the doctor's office for another thirty minutes, the doctor finally came in. He examined Heath and said he was constipated and to go ahead and give the boy an enema when I got home.

Please understand me. I had problems getting a spoonful of applesauce in his other end. I had no idea how to manage a tube in his backside.

On the way home, Heath said, "When do I get my medicine?"

"When we get home," I answered briefly. Then, feeling like I should explain, I said, "Son, you are going to get an enema instead."

"Yes!" he exclaimed. This surprised me, because the average person doesn't get very excited about a large object being placed in his backside.

I said, "Son, do you know what an enema is?"

"Of course, Dad," he answered, "and I think I want a rabbit."

I thought, A rabbit? I didn't know they came in animal shapes?

I said, "Son, what do you mean, 'a rabbit'?"

"That's the type of enema I want," Heath said. After a few seconds, I finally figured it out. "No, Heath, not an animal—an enema." He thought about that and then asked, "Can I call it Sam, like Laken's fish?"

I was going to correct him, but how do you explain the difference between an object being placed in your bottom and a bundle of fur with floppy ears? I replied, "Sure, you can call it whatever you want." Needless to say, by the end of the night, Heath was not too fond of Sam the enema.

That night, Heath informed me, "Dad, my bottom has a crack in it."

~

With our firstborn, I was one of those weird, protective dads.

~

"Of course it does, Son. Why do you say that?" I asked.

He said, "Because it leaks now."

Be Quick To Hear, Slow To Speak and Slow To Anger

In the last chapter, I talked about the languages of love and about ways to communicate with your children that will convey love and build trust in your relationship. The next step in communicating with your children is to realize that they want to be heard. Therefore, we have to learn how to be great listeners. We need to be that person they know they can come talk to about whatever is going on in their lives.

Sitting down and sharing with Dad is an experience like no other. And as dads, this is what we want for our children. We want them to think, Dad seems to know what to say and when to say it. He guides me lovingly when I need it, and he just listens lovingly when I need it. He demonstrates a heart of compassion for even the little things in my life that are big to me. Going to Dad isn't something I do only when I have nowhere else to turn. Instead, it's something I love to do whenever I get the chance.

I read a great book once that said, "So then, my beloved brethren, let every man be swift to hear, slow to speak, slow to wrath."

DAD

We must be swift, that is, always ready to hear what our children want to say. To encourage this kind of mentality in our kids, we have to become masters at listening. Listening is a skill that we have to practice. It is about learning how to hear our children's hearts, rather than just the words that come out of their mouths. It is about learning to be sensitive to the situation, knowing what to say, how to say, and when to say something. And more importantly, it's about knowing when to say nothing. You cannot be a great dad until you learn to be a great listener.

We are to be slow to speak, meaning we are to think out in our minds what we're about to say; we don't just blurt out whatever pops into our heads. Here's why: "Even a fool is thought wise if he keeps silent, and discerning if he holds his tongue."

Even a foolish dad can sound wise to his children if he keeps silent. Yes, we want to speak into their lives, but it only takes one time of opening up your mouth too quickly to sound foolish.

I know it's hard to believe, but I've been guilty of speaking too quickly at times. My son Laken, like his dad, is vertically challenged. In other words, we are quite possibly the handsomest men on the planet; but God compensated for that by making us the smallest—otherwise we would steal all the women from the rest of you. Because of my height, I know what it feels like to be made fun of in the third grade. So when Laken told me about this kid at school who was making fun of his height, passion rose up inside me. It just so happened that this kid was fat.

I, the mature dad who is writing this book on great fathering, asked my son a real character-building question: "Isn't that the big fat kid?"

Laken answered, "Yes."

"Son," I said, "it's easy to fix this problem. Every time he opens his mouth to you, call him fatty. Tell him to go eat a donut. Ask him how he can fit through the door, or how a chair can hold his big, fat butt!"

Can't you agree that this was an amazing piece of advice? Some could argue it was God-inspired.

Everything was fine afterward, and the problem was solved—until Laken told Mom about my "inspired" idea. For whatever reason, Mom didn't find it to be a helpful—I believe the actual word she used was intelligent—solution to the problem. So the two of us came up with a better plan—one that applied some character—to resolve the problem.

You see, in advising Laken, I had allowed some of my own junk to creep in—all because I didn't fully think it through before I spoke it out. I wasn't slow to speak.

DAD

My dad always used to say, "Be slow to anger." There will be times when your kids come to you with a problem. And it makes you so mad that they got themselves into that situation. But because you want to keep them coming back, you practice being slow to anger.

Let me give you an example. Once when I was nineteen years old, my father got a call from me at two in the morning. "Dad, can you come and pick me up?"

"Car break down?" he asked.

I replied, "No."

"Have you been in an accident—are you all right?"

"No, Dad. I'm fine. I just need a ride."

At that point, he knew that I was a little drunk and had no other way home but to drive myself. (It was one of three total times I drank in my life, but I thought I had to try it.) He came and picked me up. He asked about my night but said nothing about my being drunk.

The next morning, I apologized as we went to pick up my car. He said "I would much rather pick you up than have you risk your life and drive." And that was all we ever said about it. He could have gone off on me and let me know how disappointed he was in me. He could have grounded me. But he didn't. He did, however, open the door for me in the future to keep coming to him. And I learned my lesson without a lecture.

I had allowed some of my own junk to creep in.

DAD

Your mindset has to be, How can I convey a solution and get my children on the right path without damaging the trust? For your kids to come to you with a problem at all is trust. But if coming to you means facing a huge negative consequence, such as a screaming session, then the next time, they won't come to you at all. You just lost the opportunity to speak into their lives.

If my father had gone off on me the night I called him, then maybe the next time, I would have tried to drive myself home. I could have gotten in an accident, hurting myself and maybe someone else, too. And maybe later in life, when I had an emergency, I probably wouldn't have gone to Dad because that would have meant listening to a big lecture. Would you call your dad under such circumstances—I know I wouldn't!

Quick to hear, slow to speak, and slow to anger.

Characteristics of a Bad Listener

We know it's important to listen to our kids, but we don't always know how to develop those listening skills. Sometimes it helps to know what bad habits we need to avoid before we can learn good habits. So let me give you some characteristics of a bad listener in order to show you by contrast how to be a good listener. We all possess at least one of these negative traits. Identify yours, and you will know what you need to work on.

The Comparers

The first characteristic of a bad listener is comparing. If you're a comparer, while someone is talking to you, you will compare yourself to them. Maybe you'll compare that person's hardships with yours. It's like the dad who says, "Son, I know you think your life is hard, but when I was a kid, I walked ten miles to school…in the snow…uphill…both ways…barefoot! I once even killed a bear with a loose-leaf notebook. So what I'm saying to you is, 'Be happy.' Your life isn't that hard."

Think about it. If you have a problem, you don't like to think that your problem is less important than the person's you're talking to. It's as if that person is saying, "Your problem is not big enough for me to listen to." And you don't want your child to feel that way, either—to walk away thinking, If my problem isn't important to my dad, am I important?

My father, whom I brag about throughout this book, did this exact thing one time in my life. So I can talk about this based on experience. Of course, my father waited until I was thirty-four years old to do it, not when I was a child, but it still made me mad!

I had just had knee surgery, one of the big replacement surgeries. I was at home recovering and had gotten up to go to the bathroom, not realizing the effect the pressure of the pooling blood and my weight would have on my knee. By the time I had hobbled to the bathroom, I was in a cold sweat from head to toe, and the pain just kept getting worse and worse until I wanted only to go home to Jesus. I hobbled back to the couch, where I lay, screaming in pain. I started popping pain pills like Chiclets, but they were useless.

Holly called my dad and asked him to come over and watch me so she could go pick me up some stronger drugs. I told her to find some guy on the street—I didn't care—as long as she got me some drugs!

So there I was, lying on the couch, close to tears from the worse pain I have ever experienced in my life. In my drugged-up state of pain and madness, I remember my father looking at me and saying, "Son, you haven't had pain until you've had a kidney stone. They say the only pain comparable to a kidney stone is childbirth."

At that point, my wife said, "Yes, your knee pain is nothing compared to childbirth."

And my father chimed in again, "Son, take this pain and multiply it by two at least, and that is what kidney pain feels like."

If I could have reached my crutches, I think I would have attacked them both.

The point is, don't ever discount the emotional needs of your child by exaggerating your own pains in hopes of lessening his or hers. It doesn't work, and it communicates a lack of concern. Now, stories of your past hurts and pains that are similar to theirs sometimes do help. Growing up, when a girl broke my heart, it was cool to hear stories of how my mother had broken my dad's heart off and on.

Let me share my favorite story. My dad was in the Navy and was docked in Italy. My mother was a senior in high school at the time and had asked Dad to take her to the prom. My dad had to pull hundreds of strings to get the time off. He paid $650, which back in the '60s was a lot of money, to fly fifteen hours to Minnesota. From there, he took a four-hour bus ride, went to the dance, and then traveled another twenty hours back to the ship. Waiting for him at the ship when he arrived back was a "Dear John" letter saying she wanted to break up with him. Now that is funny!

My dad's pain wasn't worse than mine, nor was his experience. It was kind of the same. And it made me feel like I wasn't the only one to go through something like that.

The Pretenders

I shared about the comparers. What about the pretend listener? That is the next characteristic of a bad listener. It also can be used to describe me at times. But it's not my fault! (And, you know, that statement goes

> Don't ever discount the emotional needs of your child by exaggerating your own pains in hopes of lessening his or hers.

against everything I preach and believe.) Seriously, I could be at home for hours, sitting on the couch with my wife, and the conversation could be just a light, surface conversation. I'm watching the football game, and we're talking during commercials, just having a special time of togetherness. But now, with only two minutes left in the game, and Green Bay is driving for the go-ahead touchdown, at that very moment, some chemical is released in my wife's bloodstream that drives her to share from the deepest resources of her heart.

I want to be the great husband who listens and cares, but mainly I'm thinking, Why now? Why couldn't we have had this conversation sometime in the last two hours? I now have to turn my head and pretend to listen to her, nod my head, and say things like, "Yes," or "That's good," or "Hmmm…" all while taking in the game.

And then at the end of the conversation, she asks, "What would you do?" Well, since I didn't hear one single word she said, I have to say, "Honey, I think you handled it right."

"But I didn't do anything yet!" she says.

"Yes…uh…no…uh, of course not," I fumbled. "What I meant was, what you said you thought you should do is what I think you should do." She says, "Do you really think so? I mean, it will cost a lot of money."

Now she has my attention. "Actually, no, I don't think that is the answer! I think I need some time to pray about it" (whatever "it" is).

As dads, we have to learn how to focus on a conversation. And it's hard to do because we aren't like women, who are multitasking wizards. We can do about one thing at a time. But I watch my wife in sheer amazement: She can be changing the baby, cooking dinner, helping a kid with homework, talking on the phone, and putting a puzzle together all at the same time. I, on the other hand, can't change the baby and answer a simple question from another child at the same time: "Can you hold on? Dad is busy! Let me finish this, and then I will answer your question."

My kids actually prey on this weakness of mine. If I'm at the computer writing, they know that Dad is an easy target. It's so weird—in the back of my mind I can hear them ask the question. I can remember answering the question, but the answer to the question doesn't register for about fifteen minutes. And my answer rarely is about what is best for the kids; it usually is about what is quietest for Dad.

Holly comes in one day and says, "Why are the kids playing in the sprinklers out back? It's freezing outside."

I look up and, sure enough, it's the middle of February and the kids are—one, running through the sprinklers and, two, naked. I go outside, and I'm mad.

"What in the world are you doing running through the sprinklers!" I shout.

"But, Dad, you said we could!"

"No, I didn't…uh, wait a minute." And in the very back of my mind, I remember something or someone coming into the office and asking something about running through the sprinklers. And I remember thinking, It will get them out of the house so I can write—that must be a God-idea, at which point, I said, "Sure, but don't get your clothes wet."

On another occasion, I was playing this horror-type video game. The kids were all in bed, lights were out, and it was Dad time. Dad is no longer Scot the Amazing Father; he is now Scot the Zombie Killer. I was so taken up with the game that when a zombie jumped out of the closet, I jumped and screamed like a little girl. Then in the near distance, I heard a louder scream. It wasn't part of the game, nor was it me screaming. It was like a kid's scream. I pulled myself out of this make-believe world and looked over to see my seven-year-old son sitting on the couch, shaking in terror.

"What are you doing out of bed?"

Laken stuttered, "D-d-daddy, you said I could sit and watch you."

I started to say, "I would never let you watch this," and then in the back of my mind, I remember a little

voice asking, "Can I watch, Dad? Can I watch, Dad?
Can I watch, Dad? Please, can I?"

Wanting that voice to stop bothering me and to
ask no more, I must have said, "Oh, sure, watch this hor-
ror-filled game so you won't be able to sleep for a week.
It's no big deal. Dad will get you into therapy to compen-
sate for his lack of ability to listen!"

It was at this point that I knew I had a problem.
So now, when someone asks me a question, I force my-
self to stop whatever I'm doing and to focus and listen.
(But thank God for TiVo!)

Remember, the point of listening is to strengthen
the relationship, so if you aren't really listening—if
you're daydreaming, thinking about something else, or
just trying to get the kids out of your hair—you're missing one of the few moments you will get in your life to
really invest in your kids.

There will come a day when the kids are grown
and out of the house, and those times they want to really
talk will be fewer. I want to grab every opportunity I
have to communicate to them that Dad is here, Dad cares,
and that what they have to say is the most important thing
in my life right now. There will be many more football
games, many more times to play video games, and a lot
more time in my life to write. But if I miss this moment
with my child, it will be gone forever.

> The point
> of listening
> is to
> strengthen
> the
> relationship.

The Mind-Readers

What about mind-readers? These are the people who try to figure out what you're going to say and then finish your thought before you get a chance to say it yourself. I sometimes have thoughts of just slapping a person who does this and saying, "Didn't see that coming, did you?"

A good listener does just that—he listens. When you do the mind-reading thing, it's like you're trying to rush the conversation along as if you have other things to do that are more important. When you do this, you can't really give your child the attention needed to hear his heart. You are so busy trying to figure out what he is going to say that you miss what he is saying.

A great old proverb reads: "He who answers before listening—that is his folly and his shame."

The 'Rehearsers'

Another characteristic of bad listening is rehearsing, or coming up with a response while the other person is still speaking. How can you hear him or her if you're focused on what you're about to say next? Let the person finish his or her thought, and then take a moment to think about how to respond.

One of the biggest problems with "rehearsers" is that once they have formulated their response, they want to cut you off or hurry you through what you have to say so they can talk. When I'm around a group of people, my wife says I do this. I interrupt her story with funny, sarcastic comments, then tease her about how long her stories are. This gift of mine seems to cost me more lucky nights than any of my other great gifts. In a heated argument about this, I said, "It is my way of making your stories interesting" (which was a lie, but it did start the "Great Breast Embargo of 2002"). Rather than listening to you, "rehearsers" will have you listening to them.

The Wanderers

Then there are those who filter conversation, meaning they examine what you're saying to see only how it affects them. Once they realize it is safe—that you're not saying anything that interests them—they let their minds wander.

So maybe you're a filter listener. Maybe you listen to your son talk about school, and you notice, There's no big problem here. He's doing well in school. So you let your mind wander and start thinking about what it wants to think about. Then as your child continues to talk, you start wondering, for example, how the Dallas Cowboys are going to do tonight. Off your mind goes. You never hear the whole conversation; you filter through only those things that matter to you.

The Dreamers

What about dreamers? This is the listening trait of those people who "drift off" while you talk. My mom, who is responsible for most of this material on listening, was a dreamer type of listener at one time. She has since fixed the problem, but it used to be quite annoying. You could be standing there talking to her, then look at her, and see that her eyes were sort of fixed and glazed over. Mom was somewhere else. My favorite thing to do was to say the most outrageous things I could think of until she snapped out of it. For example, I'd say, "Yeah, so there I was, naked, drunk, and buying cocaine from this dealer when he pulled a gun…"

All of a sudden, she'd say, "Naked? Why were you naked and drunk? Son, go to your room."

To be a good listener, you have to focus your mind on what your children are saying and not let your mind wander.

The Advisors

What about the great advisor? This is the type of listener who is the mighty solver of all problems. His view in life is, "Bring your problems to me, and I will solve them." If you're this type, after listening to a few sentences, you turn your attention from what is being said to solving the problem and coming up with advice. But in the meantime, you miss everything the other person has to say.

Realize that every time your children come to you to talk, they aren't necessarily coming to you for advice. Sometimes they want you just to listen to their problems. Have you ever had a problem you just wanted to talk out, but the person you were talking to just wanted to blurt out all the solutions you already knew? But all you wanted was some compassion or to just "unload."

To be a good listener, a father has to be sensitive to that and learn to be quiet and wait for his kids to say, "Dad, what do you think I should do?" You will find that most of the time, when you wait, they will ask. But if you offer or force advice, they will probably resent it. No one, including yourself, likes unsolicited advice.

The Know-It-Alls

The next type of bad listener is the person who always has to be right. Nothing is more annoying than someone like that. This person may twist facts and even make up stuff in order to be right. If this is a problem with you, you first have to understand that you're human—you do make mistakes and you do not know everything.

Listen to your children, knowing that you don't have all the answers—and that your children don't expect

> *Realize that every time your children come to you to talk doesn't mean they want advice.*

you to have all the answers. Most of the time, they just want Dad to be there and to allow them to share.

Let me give you an example. After the fourth girl in my life had ripped my heart out and squashed it like guacamole, I asked my father why this kept happening to me. He paused a while and then said, "I asked my dad the same question thirty years ago and he said, 'I don't know.' And I don't know, either, but just trust that God has the right person for you."

My father didn't have an answer, nor did he fake one. He just listened and gave me some hope. Sometimes that is all we can give our children—some hope, some time with Dad and a big hug. And do you know what? That was enough for me fifteen years ago, and I'm sure it will be enough for my children.

The Contenders

Next on our list is the argumentative listener. (To me, this is another aspect of what hell will be like—there will people who just want to argue about everything.)

I remember a *Monty Python* episode in which a guy buys an argument. After paying, he is sent to a room where another guy is standing behind a counter. The main character—we'll call him Bob—walks in and says something like, "I'm here for an argument."

The guy behind the counter says, "You need to pay for that first."

Bob says, "No, I already paid."

"No, you didn't."

"Yes, I did!"

And so it goes until Bob finally says, "I paid in that room right there. I gave the money to the tall, bald guy."

The arguer at that point says, "We don't have a tall, bald guy who works here."

Bob says, "Yes, you do."

"No, we don't," and so on.

Finally, the arguer says, "Okay, time's up. Hope you got your money's worth."

Now that seems ridiculous, but have you ever tried to talk to an argumentative person? Their views and philosophies of life seem to change like the wind. It's like they look for ways to argue with you. If you say the sky is blue, they'll say it's red and then feel they must prove you wrong. They interrupt your story, either to argue facts or to tell you what you said or did wrong.

I once had a friend like this. I remember one Christmas Eve, he had just gotten laid off from his job. I said, "That really stinks! What kind of company lays people off on Christmas Eve?" (That seemed like the right response to me.)

My friend responded by saying, "Hey, the company has to do what it has to do. Besides, you don't run a company that size, so how can you judge what they do?"

"Okay, you're right," I wanted to say. "I think it's great that they laid you off on Christmas Eve, and I hope they didn't give you any severance pay, either."

My point is, do you find yourself arguing with your kids all the time? It's simply not a helpful listening technique. Remember, you can't change them until you change you. No one likes to argue, and if your kids know that every time they go talk to Dad, they end up arguing, it won't be long before they stop going to Dad. Once again, we need to practice being swift to hear, slow to speak, and slow to anger.

CHAPTER 12

IT WOULDN'T BE AN ARGUMENT IF YOU'D JUST LET ME BE RIGHT

Laken at the age five made an interesting career choice. On the news one afternoon, as he and I were headed out the door, we heard, "Tonight on 'Live at Five,' you will hear about the girl who stripped for a cop."

Laken said, "Dad, why did the lady strip for the cop?" Without thinking I said, "She wanted the cop not to give her a ticket."

"Why would the cop not give her a ticket?"

Once again without thinking, I blurted out, "Well, Son, because then she would be naked, and some guys like to see girls naked."

"Why?" he asked.

Actually, that was a good question. Why? I wondered. But then it struck me, we are headed down the dreaded and greatly feared path of the sex talk. I'm thinking, Dear Lord, I'm not prepared for this "birds and bees" talk. He's too young. I still don't even fully understand the birds and the bees. I surely don't want to give him the same talk my dad did, talking about fallopian tubes and ovaries—which was obviously his ploy to confuse me in a desperate attempt to keep me away from it all.

"Well, Laken," I almost passed out at this point, "guys like…uh…guys have…uh," and then I thought of an example that I felt was from God. Without thinking it through, I blurted out, "Well, why do you like to play with your Batman?"

Right then, I knew I hadn't thought that through enough. I said, howbeit too late, "Never mind that ex-ample." But very quickly, Laken asked, "Does the cop like to play with her?"

"No, Laken. Well, maybe—but that's another sub-ject. God made man to…when he gets married…"

"Are they married?" he interrupted. "No, son, they're not! I wish they were, but they're not." Then I just said it: "God just made us to like to see girls naked. Get in the van!"

Laken seemed to accept this, and I thought I was out of the woods. We got in the van, and as we were driving, I heard him say, "Dad?" I ignored him, hoping he would leave me alone.

"DAD!"

"DAD!"

"DAD!"

"DAD!"

"What, what, what, what, Laken?"

"Do you like to see Mommy naked?" (I lost consciousness for a while.) I said, "Well, yeah, Dad enjoys a peak every once in awhile." Then came the ever-evil question: "Why?"

"Uhhhh…" (long uncomfortable pause.)

"Is it because of her boobies?" he offered. I was praying, God, please take me home now. I never asked for the Rapture before, but now is the time. My mind was racing, and I thought about just putting the van in the ditch. Finally, I said, "Sure, Laken, Dad likes her boobies."

"Dad, when do I get to see girls naked?"

I said quickly, "Son, not for a long, long time—not until you are married, which won't be for a long time."

Again, the dreaded question: "Why?"

"Well, Son," I replied, "because you have to grow up. And besides, Dad wants you to live with him for awhile, because when you get married, you have to get your own house."

Laken exclaimed, "Daaaaad! Come on! I don't have money for a house."

I said, "You have to get a job."

Laken replied, "I don't want to get a job."

At this point I'm thinking, Great, I'm raising a lazy pervert. This made me mad. I blurted out,

> Then I just said it: "God just made us to like to see girls naked. Get in the van!"

"You have to have a job to get money! And you're going to get a job!"

"Dad, I think I'll just use your money."

"No, Son. I promise you, you will get a job. You will work hard at this job!"

"Dad, what if I just use Uncle Ryan's money. He's rich."

"No, no, no. You will get a job, and you will earn your own money. You won't be a freeloader, not in my house!"

"What will I do, Dad?"

Ah-ha! That was one of those training moments for Dad. Highly trained dads look for these moments because it is a time in which we can instill wisdom and biblical principles into the hearts of our children. "Laken," I said with excitement in my voice, "you can do whatever you want to do, be whatever you want to be. Whatever you put your mind to, you can do. Son, what do you want to be when you grow up?"

Without any hesitation, he replied, "I want to be a cop!"

Groan. Sighing, I continued driving—between the ditches—deciding that neither my son's career choice at the age of five, nor his endless embarrassing questions, was worth ruining a perfectly good van or a perfectly good relationship. Laken would have plenty of time to change his mind. (About being a cop, that is—not about seeing his wife naked when the time for marriage comes. That desire, I'm sure, will remain with him into old age.) But in the meantime, it feels good to know that he won't change his mind about his friendship with me. Laken will know that he can talk to Dad freely whenever he wants to and that I'll be there listening as he shares his heart with me.

Broken Relationships—The High Cost of Arguing

We've been looking at what it takes to be a great listener by looking at some of the characteristics of a bad listener. In the last chapter, we left off talking about the "contenders," those who always want to argue. If your goal is building relationships instead of tearing them down, arguing is a useless tool for communicating. An old proverb says, "The wise woman builds her house but the foolish pulls it down with her hands." If you want to play the fool and tear down the relationships in your life, particularly those with your children, you are certainly free to do it. But why not build those relationships by doing things the right way?

In this chapter, I want to explore the dangers of arguing and disputing with others.

When you argue, dispute, quarrel, or fight—whatever you want to call it—you are getting into strife and opening your life up to a lot of negative results. When you argue ninety-nine percent of the time, nothing good comes out of it.

When I was student-teaching, the school superintendent came by one day to shoot the breeze with my supervising teacher. Now, I was a math major, and I knew my math. I was at the top of my class and pulled straight A's in all of my classes. My teacher was a math teacher, and he knew his math, too.

During the conversation, the superintendent was trying to impress us, talking about some equation he was using to figure out the gallons of water in his pool. But he was wrong. I was 100 percent sure he was wrong. So I, being the twenty-two-year-old know-it-all, said, "No, that's not how it goes."

Of course, he said, "Yes, it is."

I responded, "No, you're close but this is how it goes."

He said, "Son, I was doing math when you were still in diapers."

I protested, "Honestly, Sir, that is not right." I then turned to my teacher and said, "Right?"

I was shocked when he said, "No, Scot, you're wrong."

When the superintendent finally left, I said, "If I'm wrong, then show me that equation."

DAD

He said, "Actually, you were right, but why prove the man wrong? Why not let him save face? He didn't ask for your opinion, and, quite frankly, he didn't want it. Why argue with him? Is it going to make him like you any more? When you go to get a job, will it help you any?"

I understood my teacher's point. Sure, I was right, but how much smarter would I have been to have kept my mouth shut.

Understand this and life will be so much easier. The only way to win an argument is to avoid it. You cannot and will not ever truly win an argument.

You can't win an argument because even if you do win it, you still lose. Why? Well, let's say you win. You shoot your competitor's argument full of holes, and you prove that he is a moron and that you are the smartest man on the earth. You walk away, and he feels inferior. You have hurt his pride. He will resent your triumph. You won but you may not have changed anything. That other person might still think he's right. But now he's hurt, thinking of ways to get even and to prove you wrong.

Benjamin Franklin once said, "A man convinced against his will is of the same opinion still."

What is better—to win an argument with your spouse but have her pout all night and be mad—or to

> The only way to win an argument is to avoid it.

work out the disagreement in a way that everyone wins and you still get lucky? (I honestly have learned to "throw" arguments sometimes just so I can get lucky.)

I read the following once in the Boston Journal. It said, in effect, "Here lies the body of Willey Jay, who died maintaining his right-of-way. He was right, dead right, as he sped along. But he's just as dead as if he were wrong."

How many of us have been so right that we were dead right? But now the relationship is dead, just as dead as if we were wrong. You may be right—you may be dead right as you speed along in your argument—but as far as changing another person's mind is concerned, you may end up with the same outcome as if you were wrong.

An old proverb says, in essence, that hate is never ended by more hate but by love. In other words, you will never win an argument, but you can love your way through a disagreement. Use this principle—just try it for one week. I guarantee you will then use it for life. It will take a majority of strife and anger out of your life.

Think about it. If you didn't fight or argue with anyone in your life, how much better would life be? And it would change the service you get at restaurants!

Please do not judge me on the story I'm about to share because I was young and a little ignorant. I was twenty-three years old, in fact, and ready to rule the earth. My brother, brother-in-law and I decided to go to a chicken wings restaurant. The waitress came to our table, and she was just plain mean. We tried to joke with her a little but she demanded, "Can I just get your drink order!"

So I ordered a Cherry Coke. When I got it, I took a drink, and it was about ninety percent cherry syrup and only a little coke. So I politely said, "This Coke is all cherry syrup. Could I get another one, please?"

She, with a nasty tone about her, replied, "We're not going to fill it all the way to the top because you already drank some."

That was probably the stupidest thing I have ever heard in my life. I drank about an inch of soda! I said, "Whatever. Just bring me a new one."

So by then, I was a little annoyed. Then she brought out our wings. I had ordered twenty wings, and, at that restaurant, they usually brought you one side of Ranch dressing per ten wings ordered. Well, this waitress brought me just one side of Ranch. I said, "Could I get some more Ranch?"

To which she replied, "That will cost you twenty-five cents."

Now, I had been going to that restaurant for five years and the Ranch was always free. So as she walked away, I said, "I'll just take that out of your tip—oh, wait—you aren't getting a tip."

She turned around, rushed toward me, got in my face, and just went off. "I won't take that from you! I don't need your money, you ignorant little...(blah, blah, blah)."

For a brief moment it felt like we were married. She went on like that for an uncomfortable length of time, so I picked up a menu and began to act like I was looking for something. Then I said, "Excuse me, I'm looking for the price of something."

She said, "What!"

I answered, "I'm looking for how much it would cost for you to shut your mouth. Whatever that price is, I will gladly pay it. I'll put it on a credit card, finance it. It doesn't matter what the price is—as long as it gets you to shut your trap, it's worth it." My brother and brother-in-law's chins dropped and they began laughing so hard, they fell out of their chairs. Well, this waitress had nothing to say. She stormed away, and the next thing I knew, Bruno the 300-pound chef was escorting me out of the building, telling me I was never allowed back.

Ten years later I had a similar experience with a waitress, but this time I just smiled and continued to be nice. When it came time to tip, I gave her a thirty-five percent tip and then put the church business card on the table. The next Sunday, she came up to me in church and apologized. She was having a horrible day, problems at work and at home. She has been coming to church ever since.

Those are similar situations, but they had different endings. Why? Because although I can't control another person who's being argumentative, I can control myself. In the second situation, I took control of what I could control.

Learning the dangers of arguing will change the way your boss and your co-workers treat you. It will change your friendships and your relationships. It will change your marriage and your relationships with your children.

Remember, a misunderstanding is never ended by an argument—only by love. And where your children are concerned, your job is not to argue with them. Don't fight with them to get them to do the right thing. Instead, learn to guide and direct them with your love.

I'm especially talking about not arguing with your kids later, in the teen years. Sure, there may be times you have to say, "I'm not going to argue with you. This is the way it's going to be," because that is what's best for them. For example, you're not going to let your daughter at fifteen date the bum who's eight years older. She may be upset at first, but I believe that when she calms down, then you can try to explain it to her. However, that

~

A misunderstanding is never ended by an argument.

~

doesn't mean the issue is open for negotiation. Sure, she may be upset, but in ten years, she will look back and say, "Thanks, Dad."

At age fifteen, I—like most teenagers—knew it all. And I definitely knew the right people to hang out with. There was this kid named Mike, who was one of those rebellious, cool types. He would want to ditch church and sit in the park and chew tobacco. He even brought some Jack Daniels to church in a flask. He cussed, talked dirty, and was everything I guess I wanted in a friend. My dad saw through this and said, "You're not allowed to hang out with him."

I used every argument in the book. "But, Dad, I could be a good influence on him. I could get him into church! Come on, what would Jesus do? Dad, I can get him saved." All of these arguments, of course, were made-up excuses to get my way. (The sad thing is, many parents buy into this.) The real truth was that I really wanted to hang out with this guy who was rebellious and "cool." But my father said, "No, and there will be no more arguments." The last I heard, this kid was in jail, serving a ten-year sentence.

My father never argued with me. On big issues, there was no argument. It was, "This is what we will do." On little issues, he heard my heart and communicated direction and guidance to me.

Understand that argumentative "listeners" dabble in dangerous territory, allowing themselves to be tools of the devil. Arguing rarely wins anything worth having, but it does damage the people involved.

Attributes of a Great Listener

Now that we understand many of the characteristics of a bad listener and how to avoid these pitfalls when communicating with our children, let's focus on what it takes to be a great listener. This is the listener we should determine to be in all areas of life, but most importantly with our wives and children.

A great listener first wants to understand and then he wants to be understood. He recognizes that listening is an active process, not a passive one. In other words, he knows you have to work at it to be good at it.

A great listener is mentally alert to what the other person is saying. He realizes that we were given two ears and only one mouth for a reason—so we would spend more time listening than talking.

A father who is a great listener generally does little talking but a lot of listening. A good listener sometimes plays ignorant, realizing that one of people's greatest needs is to feel important and to know things you don't know. A great listener at times acts like what his child is saying is something new and unknown to him.

"Really, Son? I didn't know that. Tell me more." Come on, who doesn't like to talk when you feel like you're the smart one in the conversation!

A great listener shows genuine interest, stops what he's doing, and focuses on what the other person is saying. He concentrates on what is being said, not on what he wants to say next, knowing that you can't listen to yourself and to the other person at the same time.

A great listener doesn't jump to conclusions; instead, he lets the person paint the entire picture. A great listener motivates the other person to say more and uses verbal rewards that make him or her want to talk to him again. A father who is a great listener might say, "Son, that was an amazing story. You have a gift for telling great stories." This father knows that any behavior he reinforces, his children are guaranteed to repeat, and he wants his children to talk to him.

A good listener uses what is called the silent pause. Nobody likes dead time or quiet gaps in the flow of the conversation but a good listener tries to allow the other person to fill them. Oftentimes, that gets the wheels of conversation going again.

A great listener listens to what the person is trying to say, not just the words being said. He looks for nonverbal clues and tries to read between the lines. He takes out all the fluff and other junk and looks at what the person really is trying to convey—sometimes by what the person is not saying. A great listener listens with genuine compassion and puts himself in the other person's shoes. He tries to feel what the other person feels.

A great father does all of these things, and he focuses on setting up situations to talk. Once a month, he takes his daughter out on a date when just Dad and daughter go to dinner, and he lets her share her heart. A great father takes his son on a walk, on a bike ride, or fishing together. He looks for whatever activity he can come up with—it could be as simple as saying, "I'm going to put some gas in the car. Why don't you ride along?" He just carved out of twenty minutes of priceless conversation time with his child.

Becoming a great listener to your kids is simple. Remember, your goal isn't to talk, but to listen. And by showing them the importance of listening, you train your kids how to communicate in relationships in the future.

So become swift to hear, slow to speak, and slow to anger. In other words, become a master listener, some-one your children will come to in order to share their hearts—now and for the rest of their lives.

> A great listener doesn't jump to conclusions; instead, he lets the person paint the entire picture.

CHAPTER 13

YOUR CHILD'S SECRET PLACE

Once when I was eight years old, I went out and watched my dad clean the garage. This surprised him because watching him clean had never interested me before. He said, "What are you doing?"

"Nothing," I answered. He stopped cleaning and said, "Come over here and sit by Dad." We began to talk about marbles, baseball and the *Six Million Dollar Man*.

Finally, I worked up the courage to say, "Dad, I'm going to burn in hell."

This shocked the heck out of him, but he calmly asked, "Why do you think that?"

I began to tell him that about a month before, my Sunday school teacher had said that if you lied, you would go to hell. By the age of eight, I figured I had made up enough lies to be put in charge of hell! My dad went on to share with me how that wasn't what the Bible said.

At that time in my life, I opened up a part of my heart that no one could get into without my permission. It was the first time I remember doing so. I was a little scared because that area of my heart was so fragile. With my actions, I was saying, Dad, come into my heart, and I hope I can trust you. Dad saw the opportunity, which could have been easily missed if he'd said a simple, "Why don't you go off and play and let Dad clean the garage?" But he saw the opportunity, came into my private world, and left my heart in better condition than it was before. It took a great deal of trust to open up this fragile place to him, and had he not treated it right, he would have broken my trust. And there would have been a great chance he would never have seen that part of my heart again.

For the next few years, there were countless more times I opened up that part of my heart to him. But here are a few of my more memorable ones.

I was ten years old, and Dad was tucking me into bed. He sensed something in me. It was like I wanted him to stay at my side and talk, although I wasn't saying anything. He seemed to understand this and said, "Son, come with me. Let's have a bowl of cereal."

We sat down in the kitchen and began to talk about soccer, school, and Arthur Fonzerelli—"The Fonz." Finally, I got up the courage to say, "Dad, I think I have cancer."

He answered, "So when do we start chemo?" I'm sure he wondered when I had gotten my medical degree. I began to explain that my Sunday School teacher had said that if you confess something, it would happen.

Well, the year before, we were playing doctor, and I had said that I had cancer and needed an operation. I had confessed it, so I figured now I must have it.

Once again, I said, Dad, come into my heart. I'm still a little scared because it is fragile. But I trusted you before and I hope I can trust you again. Dad saw the opportunity, which could have been easily missed with a simple kiss on the forehead and the words, "Come on, now. Go to sleep." But he saw the opportunity, came into my private, inner world, and left my heart in better condition than it was before. It took a great deal of trust to open up this fragile place to him, and had he not treated it right, he would have broken my trust. There would have been a great chance he would never have seen that part of my heart again.

I was fourteen years old when I went out one day and watched Dad work on the car. This surprised him, because changing plugs in a vehicle had never interested me before. He said, "What are you doing?"

"Nothing," I answered. "I just thought I would come out and watch."

He stopped what he was doing and said, "Let's go get a root beer real quick."

I said, "Sounds good."

We got our root beers and sat down. We started talking about soccer, school, and *The Dukes of Hazard*.

> Had he not treated it right, he would have broken my trust.

After a few moments of silence, I finally got up the courage to say, "Dad, I have trouble talking to girls."

For the next hour and a half, I shared my heart with my dad. For the next hour and half, I allowed my father into a place of my heart that no one can get to except by invitation. Dad saw the opportunity, which could have been easily missed with a thoughtless, "Why don't you go inside and watch some television and let Dad finish fixing the car?" Instead he saw the opportunity, came into my private world, and left my heart in better condition than it was before. It took a great deal of trust to open up this fragile place to him, and had he not treated it right, he would have broken my trust. And there would have been a great chance he would never have seen that part of my heart again.

I was nineteen years old. I went out and started helping Dad with the lawn. This, he knew, was one of the great signs that Jesus was coming back soon. Dad stopped the mower and said, "Hey, let's go get a root beer."

We got our root beers and started talking about college, weightlifting, and the TV show *Cheers*. I began to tell him about the girl I almost slept with the night before (my Sunday School teacher; okay, that is a joke). I shared the pressures I was feeling from the relationship.

By now, opening up my heart to my dad was easy. I knew I could trust him. Dad saw the opportunity, which could have been easily missed with a, "Grab the Weed-Eater and get after that grass!" But as always, he saw the opportunity, came into my private world, and left my heart in better condition than it was before. By this time I knew that if I could trust my dad with the innermost secrets of my heart, I could trust him with anything.

To build a trusting relationship with our children, we need to understand and respect our children's secret world.

Our Three Worlds

We all live in three worlds. We have our public world; that is where you spend most of your time with people—maybe those at work, church, or the fitness club. You know each other, but not very closely. You are friendly to one another—you may say hi and you may talk a little about surface things, like the weather, sports, or church. But outside of small talk, those people don't really know you. That is the public world.

We also all have an individual world. The individual world involves family and close friends. In this realm, you share a little more about yourself and what is going on in your life. You share the little problems, the little concerns, you have. You share the "surface" of your heart with these people.

Under the surface is a third world we live in. There, we have what we could call the "closet." You have some skeletons in that closet that you can't share with just anyone, or maybe there is no one you feel you can share these skeletons with. It's a place where you keep your personal thoughts, big wishes, and hopeful dreams. In there lie the big concerns of life, things you don't like about yourself, your insecurities, fears, and anxieties. It's where you store those memories you're embarrassed or feel guilty about. (I, of course, put all of mine in this book.) There are things in there you don't feel you can trust with just anyone. My question to you is this: Do your children trust you enough to let you into their closet?

Your private, inner world is the most secret of all places. No one can visit your private world without an invitation. Therefore, you will never know what your children are thinking unless they let you into that world.

Your child has a private world that is constantly changing. Things that concerned you when you were sixteen are no longer part of that world by the time you're eighteen. Being scared of going to hell was soon not part of that world for me. My worrying about talking to girls was soon no longer part of that world.

You see, what's in there is not as important as how we as parents treat the contents of that heart.

Watch for the Open Window

Fathers need to be sensitive to this secret world. We need to know when our children are ready to open up that world. We should always be looking for it, because that window only opens for a moment. And if you miss it, that chance may be gone forever.

You see, the window isn't always open, and you can't open it on your own. Your child wants to open it, but needs you to want to come in. If you act busy, if you don't see it, the child goes away and closes that window. And that topic more than likely will never be available again.

I hope you are seeing the importance of this.

The window opens at the weirdest times. Maybe it opens when you're taking a walk or tucking your kids into bed. You could be cleaning the garage, mowing the lawn, or watching TV. And it is almost always awkward. The child just comes and stands near you. He may help you do something that normally he doesn't do. Or she may want to go with you to the store or ride with you on an errand. What can happen is, if you don't know what to look for, you can easily miss that open window.

It would be easy to say, "Hey, why don't you go off and play? Let Dad work on this by himself," or, "Dad has to do some quick errands by himself." But if you do—just like that—you missed it. You missed your child

> That window only opens for a moment. And if you miss it, that chance may be gone forever.

opening up the window of his heart and saying, Dad, come on in. I want to give you a little glimpse of something that is on the inside, something in my private world. I'm taking a chance, Daddy, because no one has access to this world unless I invite him. Can I trust you?

I challenge you to look for this open window into your child's secret world. Anytime your child is hanging around, maybe even doing something awkward around you, pay attention. Do what my father did. Stop what you're doing and give your son or daughter the opportunity to let you in. You will be building trust in them and in the relationship. If your children can trust you with what's going on inside, then they can trust you with everything else.

Since you want your kids to open up their hearts—and for the rest of their lives to keep opening up to you—you have to be very gentle and careful with what you do and say inside their secret world. If you condemn them, put them down, or act like their concerns are no big deal, you might just close this window forever. Sure, you can still have a relationship with your child, but it will never be as close as the relationship that is allowed in the secret world.

Suppose your son comes to you and says, "Dad, I'm having trouble talking to girls," and you say, "Don't be silly! It's no big deal to talk to them. Why are you worried about it, anyway? You're too young to be thinking about that." You just went into that window like a bull in a china shop, knocking everything over, saying what he's feeling is stupid nonsense and a waste of your time. Your child will walk away, thinking, I love you, Dad, but I know I can't let you in here again.

Or maybe your daughter comes and tells you about her boyfriend pressuring her to have sex. What if you go off on her, telling her she can't see him anymore, because your family has rules and regulations—and punishment. Understand that had she not opened up to you, you would have never known, and she would have ended up in bed with him. You punished her for letting you into her secret world, and guess what? You won't be let in again.

Entering your child's secret world is like visiting someone's house. If you go in and trash the place, you won't be invited back. But if you go in, make sure you don't break anything. Clean it up, and leave it better than when you got there. Then you can expect to be invited there again.

Please don't miss the window! Don't go into your children's inner world and condemn or punish them for opening it up. Instead, cherish every time and treat it like the treasure it is. Do this, and your children will be inviting you in for the rest of their lives.

DAD

I want fathers of young children to understand that you want to be there when your little ones open that window and say, "Daddy, come on in." For a little one of five, six or seven years old, their issues of life may not be very big to us, but they are major to them.

Teach your children early on that they can trust you with their innermost thoughts, questions, and problems. To build a trusting relationship, we need to realize that there is another world going on inside that little life, and once in a while, that child is saying, "Daddy, if I can trust you with my heart, I know I can trust you with anything." When children learn early that they can trust their dads with their secret world, then when they get into the teenage years, they will still say, "Dad, come on in."

Treat your children's secret world with respect so that you will always be welcomed back.

Chapter 14

Being the Source of Encouragement in Your House

Bedtime at our house is a fun little time. I remember with only the two kids how hard it was, but now with four children, it takes an act of God to get them into bed. You have to get them the drinks of water. Then you have to make the nine different bathroom trips, because they feel that if they do that long enough, they won't actually ever have to go to sleep.

On special nights, "Zabola" comes. This eases the pain, because the kids know that if they aren't in bed, quiet, with the lights off, Zabola won't show up. So Zabola knocks on their door, and they all (including the two-year-old) go, "Whooooo is it?"

With a growl, I say, "ZABOLA!"

They giggle. We repeat this three times, and then Zabola comes in and does an exaggerated tip-toe into their closet, closes the door behind him, and repeats the knocking process. Finally, Zabola jumps out of the closet, tickles them all, and then runs out of the room. Then Dad walks in and asks what happened.

By the way they answer me, I really believe they think Zabola is somebody other than me. They scream,

"Zabola was here!" Even my two year old screams, "Abola, ere, Abola ere!"

So we do Zabola, and then go through a little Bible and prayer time. Laken could pray forever, and I often actually find myself praying to God, Please make him stop. In the Name of Jesus, please God. We've prayed for everybody in India, and I wanna be done.

After prayer often comes the question, "Dad, can we go get some men, puh-l-e-e-e-a-a-se?" (Their little toy soldiers are down in the basement.)

And I say, "Yeah, if it will get you to be quiet, I don't care what you want. Go ahead and get your little men."

On one particular night, Laken and Heath go down into the basement. Baylor, who has only gone potty five times that night, has to go again. So Baylor goes off to the bathroom, and when he comes out, he walks to the edge of the steps to the basement and stops.

Baylor says, "Dad, I'm scared."

Now, I realize that the great dad writing this book should go down with him, but at times, I'm the lazy dad who doesn't want to go down into the basement. I say, "Son, there is nothing to be scared of. Go get your men."

But Baylor insists. "Dad, I am scared. Can you go with me?"

Since I don't want my kids to give in to their fears, I say, "You know what, Baylor, you're a little girl," and I push him down the steps while screaming, "Time to grow up, Baby Boy!" (I'm kidding. I didn't do that!)

I patiently explain to him, "Dad is right here. I am at the top of the stairs, and there's nothing to worry about." So down the steps he went.

By that time, I should have seen something coming. For one, Laken and Heath had been down in the basement for a long time, and they were quiet. Also, all the lights were off.

So there goes poor, innocent Baylor down the steps in the dark. Now, at the bottom of the steps, unbeknownst to Baylor and me, are my two eldest children, in whom I have instilled how to love others. For the past eight years, I have laid down my life for these children. I have "sweat blood" trying to teach them godly principles. (So please, God, help them get it right.)

All of a sudden these two children of mine jump out at my youngest son, yelling, "RO-O-O-A-AR!"

And here comes Baylor, screaming up the steps. Thanks, guys, I think to myself. Now Baylor won't be sleeping this month. I'm holding Baylor while he's screaming and crying, and I'm trying to settle him down. All the while, my two oldest children, who

~

I should have seen something coming. For one, Laken and Heath had been down in the basement for a long time.

~

don't know I'm at the top of the steps, are saying, "Baylor, why don't you come back down? It's safe now," in this sadistic tone.

By this time, I'm a little angry, and I don't do what a good father would do, because I don't always do that. What I do is—and don't judge me on this, please, because you may have thought about doing something similar—I get a blanket and put it over my head. I turn out all the lights in the house, and now it's really dark. I mutter to myself, "You guys want to dance? Let's dance with Dad a little bit. If Baylor's going to be up tonight, we're all going to be up tonight!"

I grab Baylor's little hand, and we charge down the steps. All of sudden, when we get to the bottom of the stairs, Laken and Heath jump out and yell, "RO-O-O-A-AR!"

As loudly as I can, I yell, "RO-O-O-O-A-A-ARR!!!"

Laken and Heath fall backwards, trying to get away. As I flip on the light and take off the blanket, Laken says, "Dad, I can't believe you did that to us."

I say, "You did it to Baylor!"

He says, "Yeah, but we're not Dad. Dads don't do scary things." Apparently, in my house, they do.

One of the biggest things we have to learn to communicate to our children is encouragement—something I did not do in the preceding story!

**We Must Contradict the Voices
of Discouragement From the World**

We need to be a source of encouragement in our children's lives. Kids will receive enough discouragement from society. They will be teased, made fun of, told they are "less than" or "not good enough." Society will point out and focus on their little imperfections. We all have a few characteristics that by the world's standards aren't normal, but being successful in knowing who you are comes by focusing on the great gifts and talents you do have.

As dads, it is our job to point our children to all the wonderful gifts and talents they possess. We should communicate this to them every day. We are the primary source of our children's self-confidence. We build it with the words, actions and beliefs we communicate to our children.

What a tragedy it is when a father is on the same level as the world, pointing out his child's weaknesses, with no solution on how to turn them into strengths, and tearing down a child's self-confidence rather than building it up. This father puts his child at an emotional disadvantage and even handicaps him.

The Bible talks about the kind of person who does this: "It would be better for him if a millstone were hung around his neck, and he were thrown into the sea, than that he should offend one of these little ones." I don't know what a millstone is, but I do know I don't want one hung around my neck as I'm being thrown into the sea!

Fathers should build their children up. They should be that voice inside them that says, "You can do anything you set your mind to; you are not less than; you are great looking, smart, fun; you have a great personality."

You see, when these truths—this belief system—are in their hearts as children, they become adults who are still able to say, "I can do anything I set my mind to. I'm not less than. I'm great looking, smart, fun, and I have a great personality."

What voice do your children hear? Do your voice and actions communicate to them the truths of life or the lies of the world?

Take the time to point out the gifts and talents of your children. There is nothing wrong with telling your son he is handsome and that all the girls will be after him. And you make sure you let your little girl know she is a princess and that she is the most beautiful girl in the world. Try to say it in a way that's not just flattery, but that really speaks truth from your heart about the positive characteristics of your children.

Your children hear these words in the back of their heads when the world is talking to them. When the world says they're ugly and no one likes them, they know that Dad says they're attractive, have a great personality, and make people laugh. At that point, the trust level of the relationship kicks in, and the success of that relationship will determine whose words are true to them—their dad's or the world's.

I have to give you the perfect illustration of what I mean. Laken was four years old at the time and loved to play video games. I had just bought the game "Crazy Taxi." It's a fun game in which you pick up pedestrians and then break every law known to man as you try to get them to their destination. (It's also a great character-building game for a four year-old.)

One day, as I was walking by the room where Laken was playing, I heard him yelling at the TV. I stopped and listened. He kept saying, "I don't suck. You suck."

I thought my son was hearing voices and, worst of all, talking to them. As I got closer, I heard a voice from the game say, "You suck—I'm outta' here!" and the guy in the cab jumps out of the car because Laken was taking too long. Laken screamed, "I don't suck! You suck!" What made it funny was he honestly was mad that the game would say that to him.

Later in life when the mean world says, in essence, "You suck," I want Laken to still have that same

There is nothing wrong with telling your son he is handsome.

confidence: "No, I don't suck. You suck." Even if all the world says he's a nobody, I want Dad's words speaking to him. I want all my kids to say, "My dad would never lie to me. I don't suck, and I'm not a nobody. I must be attractive, and I must have a great personality—because my father says so!"

Do you see the power of your words in the lives of your children?

You Create or Destroy Self-Esteem With Your Words

Moms tend to be the ones doing all the encouraging. And children like that. But there's just something different and very special when Dad says something encouraging. I don't know why or what the psychological reason is behind it; I just know it's true. Maybe it has something to do with agreement, because when moms and dads come into agreement, there is power behind that. Whatever the case, Mom's words are good, and kids love that she encourages them. But Dad's words seem to bring change inside a child. That change within them produces change outside of them.

As a dad, your job is to help your kids find the talents and gifts they possess inside. The great thing about this is that it takes just a few moments a day. It just takes a dad becoming aware of the power of words.

There are some things you can do. For one, make sure every day that you tell your child how awesome he or she is. Once again, it's not flattery but if you look for it, the moment that's right for a true compliment will come up.

Laken came home from school one day and said, "Dad, I got a hundred on my spelling test."

I said, "Well, that hard work you did studying, and the fact that you're a genius, really paid off!"

There were two encouraging aspects to my statement. One, I pointed Laken to the truth that hard work does pay off. If you want something, you have to work for it. Two, on the tail end, I added a little extra to his heart: "You're a genius."

An old proverb says, "For as he [a person] thinks in his heart, so is he…" There's a principle here: As your daughter thinks she's pretty and has a great personality, what is within her, in her heart, produces something around her. She believes these things, and they become true.

It is an interesting phenomenon that if we hear something long enough, after a time, we will believe it. "How is my handsome boy doing?" you can say, or, "How did you get so smart?" Here are a couple more: "How come you're so good-looking? No wonder all the girls like you!" and, "I have the best children in the world."

I started saying these things to my children at birth. Over and over, I'm programming the message the "recorder" will play in their minds. You know that re-corder I'm talking about—the one that tells you whether or not you can do something, the one that tells you if you're attractive and personable or not. It's that little recorder we call self-esteem.

Don't ask me how we got this started, but this is how we say goodbye, goodnight, or even thank you in our house. Laken, Heath, and Baylor say, for example, "Bye, Mom and Dad. You're the best mom and dad in the world." Even our twenty month-old tries, "Byeee Mom ant Dad urdbest intl wrd."

We answer, "Bye, Laken, you're the best Laken in the world. Bye, Heath, you're the best Heath…," and so on. What are we doing? We're programming their hearts, one, to look for the good in their parents, and, two, to see the good inside them-selves.

If you look for the moment to encourage your kids, you will see it. But if you're not aware, you'll miss it. And then your children only get to hear what the world thinks and believes. And, sadly, that will then become what they think and believe.

Elevate the Good in Your Children

So tell your children how blessed you are to have kids like them. Look for areas in which you can express how proud you are of them. You know, in our society, we get so caught up in suppressing the bad in our kids that we miss elevating the good.

For example, you could say, "Son, I'm so proud of the way you treated your sister back there." You just elevated the good in him, and just to hear those words again, your son will look for an opportunity to make you proud. He'll start thinking, How can I do that for my sister again? You see, you didn't have to discipline him to treat her right; you just had to notice and encourage him when he treated her right.

The other day Baylor had "Grandma time." Now, time with Grandma consists of taking the grandkids out for ice cream, candy, treats, and toys. I try to explain to my children that this is not the woman I grew up with. I tell them, "You don't realize what we had to do just to get a Happy Meal." Needless to say, Grandma time is a real treat.

Well, after Grandma time, Baylor comes home with an awesome gift that he'd gotten for his birthday just three weeks before. I said, "Son, you already have one of these."

He replied, "I know, Dad. But Laken wanted the one I got, so I got him one."

If you look for the moment to encourage your kids, you will see it.

That right there was one of the truest acts of kindness I have ever seen. He gave up his toy to bless his brother. I hugged him and went around telling everyone what he'd done and how proud I was of him. The next day, I took him out and blessed him with another toy. I wanted to so elevate that good that he'd done that he keeps on doing it.

Think back in your own life to the times your dad said to you, "I'm so proud of you." It brings back a tingle inside of you, doesn't it? For some who never heard those words, what would you give to have heard your father say that to you?

So look for areas to be proud of and then announce them to the world. It's one thing to say you're proud to your child, but it's another thing to tell those around you in front of your child. Doing that reinforces your belief in him.

Even as an adult, when my dad tells someone how proud he is of me, it makes my heart skip a beat. It puts a big smile on my face. If Dad is proud of me, who cares what the world thinks!

We as fathers should elevate the good, but how do we encourage children about their weaknesses? It depends on the weakness.

I think one of the greatest things my dad communicated to me was what we call the "Serenity Prayer," which, in effect, asks God to help us change the things we have the power to change and to help us change our attitude toward the things we can't change. That is so wise, I'll say it again: We need to learn to change those things we have the power to change, and change our attitude toward those things we can't change.

Teach your children this principle. Let me give you an example of how to do it. When Laken started baseball, like all dads, I thought he was going to be the best. Come to find out, because I waited until he was nine to get him in baseball, he was a little behind the curve.

On the way home from one particular practice, I pointed out the two good things he did and didn't mention the 100 mistakes. Every night after that, he and I worked on baseball for twenty minutes. The first three games, he struck out every time at bat. He would get frustrated, and say, "I'm no good!"

But in the Anderson house, those words are not allowed. "Son," I'd say, "you are very good. You are good at whatever you work at. We just need to practice some more this week. But remember that catch you made? That was great!"

"But, Dad," he insisted, "I struck out every time."

"Well, son, remember the last game we watched on TV? Sammy Sosa, one of the greatest hitters in the world, struck out every time!"

Laken and I started going to the batting cages three times a week. By the last four games, he only struck out once. And by the next season, he was the best batter on the team, hitting .650.

In Laken's weakness, I was able to encourage him and keep his spirits up and show him that Dad is proud of who he is, no matter what happens in life. I was able to show him the benefits of hard work—that if you're not good at something, it's easy to fix. You practice until you become good. This skill will follow him into adulthood. For example, if he were to find out he's not good at marriage, rather than quit, he'll know he can read books, get tapes, and practice until he becomes good at marriage.

Now, in that account, did I once lie to Laken or give him false flattery? No, and let me tell you something. Kids can see right through that. If I had said, "Laken, you're the best baseball player in the world," he would have known that wasn't true. But I pointed him toward the good, helped him find the good, and then gave him the keys to becoming good.

You know, it's easy to become good at something when you have your father backing you up.

A Father's Love Should Be Unconditional

It is important that your kids get unconditional love from you. I love you not for what you do or don't do, but because you exist. Your children have to have this concept built into them in life. They have to know that no matter how many mistakes they make—whatever happens—your love is unconditional. There are no conditions attached. Your attitude is, "My love is for you, not for what you do. I'm proud of you no matter what."

For example, you might say to your child, "I don't like the fact that you got a D on your report card. But that doesn't change how I feel about you. I am still the most blessed man in the world to have a child like you. Though I am proud of you, there will be some changes in your study habits and fun time until those grades come up. But my love for you isn't about what you do; it is because you exist. Though the world loves you for what you do for it, at home, you will always know that Dad's arms are open to you and that I'm here for you, no matter what."

You guide your kids into success by encouraging them toward the positive and showing them the benefits of hard work. They already know their weaknesses, so what they want is for you to notice their strengths and to be there to help them with their weaknesses.

I want to always be there to help my kids with their weaknesses. One time I was trying to show off Baylor, who was three years old at the time, to my uncle by having him recite his ABCs. So Baylor goes, "A B C D E F G H I J L M..."

I stopped him and said, "Baylor, you forgot the letter K. Start again."

"Sorry, Dad," he said and then, "A B C D E F G H I J L M…"

"Baylor," I said, "you forgot the K. It is G H I J K—K! then L M and so on. So let's start at G."

"G H I J L…," he said again. I promise you, for one hour he could not get the K

Finally, he could do H I J K L…, so I said, "Let's start from the beginning." Then he left out the G. I worked with him another twenty minutes to finally get the G back, but then he was missing the K again.

I am convinced that his brain could only hold twenty-five letters. For weeks, I worked with him, and I was close to not practicing anything I'm saying in this chapter. I got so frustrated, I wanted to just "go off." Finally, Holly and I came to the conclusion that the letter K wasn't all that important. We thought he could be quite successful without it. I mean Wal-Mart is just as good as K-Mart, and 7 Eleven is fine over Circle K.

A month afterward, I was working on numbers with Baylor, and, as God is my witness, he could count to twenty but had no eleven. When I told my brother this story, he counted out the letters, and, wouldn't you know it, K is the eleventh letter! I said to my brother, "I'll bet he has no November in his months of the year. And I guess there will be no eleventh day of Christmas. As an adult, a dozen eggs will be missing number eleven. But since there would be no eleven, twelve would be eleven. So when he buys them, in his mind, there will be thirteen in the carton; hopefully, he won't feel like a thief. And what in the world will happen at eleven o'clock!"

The point of this story is that until Baylor got his K and the number eleven, we continued to praise him in the meantime in all that he did, and we focused on the twenty-five great letters he did know, not on the one he couldn't get. (But when you look at the chapters of this book, you will notice I left out the eleventh chapter. I did it for Baylor.)

Now there will be things that your children can't change. In these cases, you have to teach them to change their attitude toward it. I know what I'm talking about, being a man who is just 5'5" (the sad thing is, that is an exaggeration). Growing up, I couldn't change my height, and my father couldn't change my height. And in those years, kids can be mean.

Actually, even adults can be funny about this, as if a person's stature is the only thing people feel the freedom to make fun of to your face. At least once a month, someone I don't know at the church will come up and say, "Man, you're short!" That makes me laugh, because if I responded with, "Man, you're fat," or

"Man, you're bald," "Boy, you have a huge nose," or, "You are one ugly woman," that would devastate them. At least when you're fat, people make fun of you behind your back—your big back (come on, don't get mad—that's funny!). But when you're short, people feel free just to come out and say it.

Growing up, I could have gotten mad and thought, Why me? Poor me. Or I could be excited about who I am, what I have, and look at all my gifts and talents. With my father's direction, I chose the latter. I learned to laugh with people and to beat them to the punch on the short jokes. (Occasionally, when people commented on my height, I would commend them on their keen eyesight and outstanding observational skills.) I focused on my awesome personality and my good looks. I never allowed those things I couldn't change to attach themselves to my self-image. Today, I have a very high self-esteem (too high, my wife sometimes says). I never had any trouble getting girlfriends growing up. In fact, I actually had more girlfriends than my tall friends. Why? Because how I saw myself was how the world saw me, too.

Your children will have things about them that the world says is "less than." People who are of the world love to tear you down to build themselves up. But we as fathers have the power to help build our kids' self-esteem so that it isn't ravaged or destroyed by the world. My dad, who is 6'2", never made a big deal about my height, so it wasn't a big deal to me. He helped me with my attitude and taught me to love myself the way I am. And that is a father's responsibility to his children.

I touched on this earlier but I want to emphasize that negative talk is not allowed in our house. "I'm stupid," "I'm no good," "I can't," "I'm ugly"—those phrases aren't allowed in our house, because those phrases, if said, will in time attach to my children's self-image.

If your child says, "I stink at math," you can say, "No, you're good at math, but we just need to practice some more on multiplication." Teach your children not to say what they feel they are, but instead to say what they want to become. In time, they can actually become what they believe if their goals are reasonable and attainable, of course. If one of them feels horrible at math, he can say he is great at math. If he says it long enough, he will begin to believe it, and then what he believes inside can come out (obviously, with the help of practice and hard work).

Another example is that your daughter may not feel beautiful. But she can say that she is. Before long, she believes it, and this belief makes her treat herself like she's beautiful—maybe she'll start wearing makeup and dressing in attractive clothes or perhaps she'll style her hair—and she then becomes beautiful.

In time they can actually become what they believe.

**Treat Your Children as Valuable and Precious
and Ensure Their Success for Life**

How you feel about something determines how
you treat it. If you feel like something is beautiful and
precious, you treat it like it is. But if you think something
is ugly and old, you treat it like that.

My first car was a 1974 Ford Falcon. It had more
rust than metal on it. Parts of the floorboards were totally
rusted out, and you could literally see the road under you.
I remember being at a stop light once, looking down,
and seeing a nickel under the car. This ugly car was
mine, and I saw it like it was beautiful. I washed it (and
watched as water ran into the interior from all the holes),
and I cleaned it. Oh, I kept it so clean!

Now, my father is the Bondo© king. I promise
you, he could build an entire car body with two five-gal-
lon buckets of Bondo©. We used newspaper, paper plates,
scraps of wood, and Bondo© to patch up all the holes in
my car, and then we had it painted. When we finished,
that car looked so nice. Although underneath all the Bon-
do© and paint, it was ugly, I treated it like it was beautiful,
and it became beautiful.

It's the same with your children. How they feel
about themselves will determine what happens outside of
them. If they feel good about themselves, they will spend
time on the hair, clothes, and good grooming. As dads, it

is our job to make sure that what's in them is right. Don't allow any negative talk to come out of them; instead always point them toward the positive.

Practical Ways To Encourage Your Kids

The following are some practical things you can do that communicate love, acceptance, and encouragement to the hearts of your children.

Most kids get a note from Mom in their lunch box from time to time. But what if once a week, you wrote a note to your child? Tell him how proud you are and that you hope he has a great day.

Think about yourself. Wouldn't you give anything if you had just one note from your father that said, "I'm proud of you, Son?" It takes thirty seconds of your time to write, but the memory and effects last a lifetime. Your children will open that note up at school, and they'll feel like they can take on the world. A note from Mom makes for a nice moment in the day, but a note from Dad can make the whole day.

Another thing you can do is write a letter to your child on birthdays and holidays. Your children get cards and letters from friends and relatives, and these cards are nice. But they shortly get tossed in the trash. The letters from Dad, however, get placed in a special place—a special box or a folder in their closet. So on those days when they don't feel sure of themselves, when they feel life isn't going just right, they can pull those letters out and remind themselves of the security they have in Dad.

What would you give to have a letter from your dad pointing out all the things he was proud of in your life? How about a letter pointing out all the good in you? This would be truly something that even today would bring a smile to your face as you read it, and even on your worst days, that letter could make you feel good about yourself.

Another practical way to encourage your children is to plan to spend a few moments with them after a sporting event, dance recital, school play, spelling bee, or a competition or activity of whatever kind. Point out the good things they did and make them feel special about their performance.

For one, this says to the child that Dad was watching; two, it says he cares; and, three, it helps get the good thoughts in before any bad thoughts have time to take root.

Look to the positive and then point them toward practice. And make sure you take time to work with them on what is important, like in the instance of my practicing baseball with my son. I took twenty minutes a night and invested in my son's success. That is just a part of a TV show's worth of time that I invested in my son instead of just wasting it in front of a television.

Don't miss out on carving out even small amounts of meaningful time spent encouraging your kids. These few moments in the day that you invest will communicate to your child that what he's doing matters to Dad. Plus, nobody likes to stink at something. When you stink at something, it can tear down your self-image in more areas than just the event you're participating in at the moment. Don't allow your kid to be the one who can't catch or hit the ball. It took me only twenty minutes a day for a month for Laken to become very good at baseball. And the confidence that came from that month of practice showed up in many other areas of his life.

The Power of Encouragement
To Heal a Broken Heart

Make sure you are there in the times of disappointment in your kids' lives. Once again, your encouragement can head off wrong thoughts before they attach themselves to your children's self-esteem.

With every girl that broke my heart, my dad was right there. Every single time when I told him, he dropped what he was doing and said, "Let's go golfing." (No wonder I'm so good at golf today!) We would get out on the course and he would just let me share and talk. And during this time, he would very smoothly direct me away from negatives about myself. Although after the

Your encouragement can head off wrong thoughts before they attach themselves to your children's self-esteem.

golf game, I still hurt inside, I left with some hope and, as always, confidence in the love my dad had for me.

We should be our children's endless source of encouragement. With our words and our actions—cards, letters, thoughtful words and acts, and time spent together—we can be there to encourage them and to pick them up when they've fallen under the heavy weight of discouragement. We need to constantly be building their self-esteem so that they can become resilient to the pressures, criticisms and condemnation of the world.

Always see the good in your children and help them see the good themselves. Help them improve and overcome the weaknesses that they can change, and, finally, point them in the direction of success by instilling in them positive thoughts and beliefs about themselves. These thoughts and beliefs will fuel a winning self-image within them that will carry them into the great life you want for them.

CHAPTER 15

GIVE ME A HUG

Some things went wrong at home one day—terribly wrong. One of the air-conditioning units had stopped working, and I found out it was going to cost $1,200 to get it fixed. My garage door opener stopped working, and I couldn't get my car out of the garage. Then I received a letter from Satan (that's what I call my health care provider) stating they weren't going to cover $4,000 on my knee surgery. I also received a picture from the police department of me driving 36 m.p.h. in a 25 m.p.h. zone. (It was a great picture; I had 8 x 10s made.) Our dog chewed up $200 in electronics, and what really put me over the edge that day was that *Judge Judy* was a rerun. It was a frustrating day, and that is an understatement. I was a time bomb waiting to blow.

In the midst of all this, my dad, who had come over for a visit, came up behind me and gave me a big hug. I was thirty-five when this happened, yet I still cannot describe adequately what that hug meant to me. Is it enough to say that it meant everything? Although I was a grown man, that hug from my father diffused my frustration and comforted my soul. That hug lifted my spirits and empowered me.

In this short chapter, I'm going to talk about the power of healthy touch.

Fathers must realize the power that resides in their arms. As a dad, your arms can bring strength and confidence to your children in any circumstance and at any age. They can bring security and stability to any situation, and they can bring love and comfort to a hurtful time. One of the greatest needs your children have is healthy touch.

Touch oftentimes says so much more than your words could ever convey. A pat on the back says, I'm proud of you. A great big bear hug says our relationship is fun. A grip on the shoulder says, You can do it, and I'm behind you. A hug in a time of pain says he is always there and everything is going to get better. A hug in a time of worry or anxiety says there's nothing to worry about when Dad is here. A great big exuberant hug says, I missed you when you were gone, and you are an important part of my life that I can't live without. A rub on the shoulders conveys confidence and comfort.

With your arms, you can send messages all day that say to your children they can trust Dad, Dad is there for them, and he loves them.

When you hold your children, it meets special emotional needs. When that need is not met, children look to other places. If you don't hold your daughter, the wrong man may. She will get that need met one way or another. If you don't hug your son, he will get that need met in other ways. Well, he's a man, you think, and men shake hands. They don't hug. No, men may shake other men's hands, but they hug their sons. And your daughters or sons never get too old to feel the purity of love in Dad's touch.

My grandfather, my dad's dad, has been gone for some twenty years. I guarantee you that my father would give just about anything to be held again by his father. If you've lost your father or live far away from him, you probably know what I'm talking about.

Do not deny your children this most basic human need. You may protest, "Well, I'm just not a touchy type of man." Then become one. It's that simple. It's not like I'm asking you to develop a hard-to-master skill. Unless we have a physical limitation of some kind, we all have the ability to move our arms into a hugging position and then squeeze! We really don't need a seminar or six-week training course for this. Of all the sections in this book, the material contained in this one should be the easiest to master.

Or maybe your excuse is, "But my kids don't like it. They push me away." That may be what they say on the outside but on the inside, they're crying out for a touch from Dad. Your kids may push away and

Fathers must realize the power that resides in their arms.

say, "Aw, come on, Dad." But you could say something like, "Dad needs a hug." (But in pressing on,
don't be insensitive and embarrass them in front of
their friends.) You're saying that you need it but, really, they need it. In a way, you have tricked them into
allowing you to meet a need they have, yet they feel
like they've met your need.

I say to my children, "Come on and sit by Dad
during the TV show." I let them sit on my lap, or sometimes I wrestle with them. I know it's my job to make
sure my children get the touch they need in their lives.

I wonder how many children are crying out to be
held. Don't let a day go by without expressing love to
your children through healthy touch.

I give my kids a huge hug when I go to work to
say, Have a great day, and I will miss you. You are valuable to me. I give them a hug every time I get home from
work. I throw them up in the air and let them know I'm
excited to see them. And I want them to feel like seeing
Dad is a fun, happy time.

I make sure that whenever my kids do something
good, I give them verbal praise and then a squeeze on
the shoulder or pat on the back. And watching a movie
on TV with Dad is like one big dog pile. All four kids
want me to hold them, and I let them sit on my lap.
Finally, at night, I give them a big hug and a kiss good-

night. My kids get a minimum of three touches a day, but these touches will last a lifetime.

Understand that touch affects trust. Wrong touch in a relationship will immediately destroy the relationship. But right touch constantly builds trust. If you want to have a great relationship with your children, then appropriate touch has to be a part of that. I know it may seem like such a little thing, but if you add up all the little things you can do as a father, the result will be success in the relationship.

You have great power to communicate how much you love your children, and that power is in your arms.

DAD

CHAPTER 16

GET A JOB!

Laken is four years old and has just gotten the chicken pox. So Mom says he can sleep with us—that way Dad can stay awake all night enjoying his two feet of bed space. Now I feel like my wife is the only one who remembered that Laken still did the occasional bed-wetting and that she put Laken on my side for that one-and-the-same fun-filled reason.

Caught between the two of them, I am somehow finally able to go off to "sleepy land." I'm dreaming and I'm in the middle of a football game. I'm Brett Favre going for it on fourth and two. I can feel the sweat pouring from my skin. Man! I mean, I am sweating! It's almost too much sweat. I wake up and I am drenched from head to toe. I'm thinking, It's hot in this house! I'm sweating like a dog! Upon further inspection, I realize that it is not my sweat I'm feeling, but rather a bodily fluid of another kind.

I shake Laken to wake him up. I want him to see what he has done. Laken opens his eyes, feels the wet bed around him, and looks at me as if to say, Sorry, Dad. Just then, Mom wakes up and says, "What's going on?" at which point Laken cries out, "MOM! DAD 'PEED' THE BED!"

At the beginning of this book, we discussed "levels" of fathering, and I said that there are three basic levels: biological; provider and protector; and finally, our highest goal, relationship.

The first level we discussed is obvious. It is the biological level of fathering. We've all had enough sex education to understand that one. And we've discussed the final goal of the relationship level. Right now, I want to back up and talk to you about level two: the father as provider and protector (which has nothing to do with my "peeing the bed" story except that being a great father demands sacrifice—your "blood, sweat, and tears," as the saying goes!).

Understand first that each level of fathering builds on the previous level, meaning, of course, that you can't skip a level and remain on a solid foundation on which to build the relationship. Obviously, you can't get to level two—provider and protector—until you have had a child, level one. But in the same sense, you can't go to level three, relationship, until you have done level two, to provide and protect. That is what I really want to talk about in this chapter.

What do I mean when I say "provide and protect"? Here's the essence of it, the real truth that I want to get across. Get a job!

Fighting Off Bears

To be a good father, one who is developing a strong relationship with your children, you must strongly accept your role as provider and protector for your family. In this day and age, our children do not see us provide and protect like fathers used to in the "old days." I hear stories about how Grandpa would take my dad along every day to work chopping wood, cleaning the school, and hunting for food. My dad tells stories of how Grandpa once trapped and killed a bear, using only a small bag of walnuts as a lure. My father could easily visualize his dad providing and protecting for his family.

Nowadays, we leave in the morning, return at night, and what we did in between is a mystery to our children. We don't even have to go to the bank to deposit our checks—now they can be deposited directly into our accounts. Children can't as easily visualize their fathers providing and protecting like kids used to.

Try this. Ask your children what Daddy does all day. My kids don't know, either. I know my kids would say, "Dad kisses us good-bye at seven-thirty and then returns at four-thirty." What I did all day is a mystery.

The days of fighting off bears and killing our food are gone, but it doesn't lessen the importance of our children seeing and knowing Dad as the provider and protector of the home.

~ Here's the essence of it, the real truth, that I want to get across. Get a job! ~

Let Your Wife Stay Home With the Kids

Our society is slowly losing this very important part of fathering, that of provider and protector. Women are taking more and more of the providing responsibilities. Now, I'm not against women working. (I wish Holly would get a job. No! I'm only joking!) I believe women can do most, if not all things, as well or even better than men. As I already said, it is an amazing sight to see a woman multitask. As a man, I can do one thing at a time. If I'm watching football, I can't watch the game and talk. I sound like a moron: "Yes, Honey, I feel like we need to…not run on third and five. That's stupid! What? Yes, Honey, I'm paying attention to you. What I was trying to say was…no, no, not a sack! Throw the stupid ball!"

And as you know, I cannot change a diaper and answer a child's question simultaneously. Whatever the child asks, I will answer a simple yes, because I cannot do both. My wife, on the other hand, can change a diaper, cook dinner, help one child with homework, talk on the phone, watch TV, read a book, and re-stucco the house all at the same time.

I am not against women having jobs. I am, however, against women taking on the stress of providing for the family. The responsibility of having enough money in the bank to pay the bills is the husband's job. I want my wife never to have to worry about there being enough money for Christmas or a nice vacation. It is my job, one, to provide that money, and, two, to make sure she and the children have the security of knowing I will do everything I can possibly do to make it happen. If my wife wants to work, fine, but she doesn't have to.

I believe that if your wife wishes to be a stay-at-home mom, it is your job to make sure she can do it, starting today! Now, before you rip this section out of the book just to make sure the missus never reads it and gets all those "hillbilly" thoughts in her head, think about it. What better investment could you make in the lives of your children than that? Could you put a price on that? No one on this earth can be as good a mom to your kids as your wife. No one loves and cares for them like she does. To allow her to invest in them, especially for those first six years, you simply can't put a price on that.

Plus, by the time you get done paying an extra car payment and spending extra for gas, child care, extra medical expenses (because kids get sick more outside the home), extra taxes, extra clothes she needs for work, and lunches, she makes about a buck an hour!

When Mom works a job, because she is often tired when she gets home, you end up having to eat out or eat fast food more often that is less nutritious and more expensive. And is all that worth having some stranger influencing your children for over half their waking moments each day their mother works? Who is having the greatest influence on your children—Mom or the baby-sitter? Who will give greater care to your children—a baby-sitter or their mother? Who will spend more time getting them emotionally ready for the time they start going to school—a babysitter with six other kids to look after or your wife? Which relationship do you want to be stronger—the babysitter and child's or the mother and child's?

Something else to consider, is the babysitter in agreement with the discipline of the children? What is expected from the babysitter in the way of nurturing character development? What are your kids learning from their caregiver about sharing, being nice, forgiving, and not throwing temper tantrums? Parents oftentimes spend their spare time fixing babysitters' "parenting" rather than sacrificing if need be to enjoy the children they're raising.

A mom at home brings a different atmosphere into the home. When she's at home, she can invest in the kids, the house and you. If her job and purpose is being a wife and mom, life in the home is so much better. She is more emotionally available to the family. She has more energy that can be directed toward the home and family.

You see, believe it or not, a woman's energy level has a limit. If she's working a full-time job, she is going to have less time and energy to invest in you and your children. You and your children's quality of life is going to be greatly affected.

When Mom is home and has time to do things around the home, and take care of the kids, the atmosphere of the home is so much different. Things operate more smoothly, and, inside, she doesn't have the guilt that goes with dropping the kids off at daycare, missing them take their first step, missing their first words, missing out on developing the type of relationship she desires.

There is something inside a woman that desires these things. If she works, she has to put on the "supermom" hat and work the full-time job, take care of the children, take care of the home. But with this supermom hat comes all the emotional instability that goes with any of us when we are pushed to our limits.

Men of this generation are sacrificing quality of life for their family and quality of home for a few extra dollars a month. And their wives are too tired to give them the attention they need (and sex). That right there should be enough incentive to tell her to quit her job right now!

As fathers, we need to see beyond what society says is important and look at what is truly important. I'm sorry if saying this upsets you, but having a happy, ful-

Who is having the greatest influence on your children—Mom or the baby-sitter?

filled wife—you can't put a price on that. And I will tell you this much, being a stay-at-home mom is more than a full-time job.

Ask yourself: Is a bigger house worth that? No! Is a nicer car or having two cars worth that? No! Is a bigger TV and surround-sound worth that? No!

Let's look to what produces overall the best quality of life for everyone in your family and pursue that.

The *Atlanta Journal* reported that children whose mothers worked outside the home are more likely to drop out of high school. Think about it from the children's perspective. It's the difference between having the security of Mom at home when they get there or getting home to an empty house. Having that consistent presence of Mom home after school brings security and relief to their world. The world is already lonely and full of stress, but walking through those doors to a mom with a big smile and hug adds something special to their day. John Yunker, a director of guidance services in our suburban school district says, "You can't expect a child to go home by himself for several hours every day and not feel abandoned and frightened."

Also, studies have shown that mothers who work outside the home spend far less time with their toddlers working on educational skills such as reading, counting, and writing, or penmanship. What a huge advantage a child has who enters kindergarten reading and writing over the child who doesn't grasp this until first grade.

Since 1950, we have seen the number of working mothers in America increase dramatically. We also have seen crimes such as murder, rape and robbery committed by children increase by over 11,000 percent. Arrest of youngsters for use of or trafficking drugs has risen more than 4,600 percent since the 1970s.

As a father, your job is to bring financial, emotional, and physical security to your home. Whatever that means you have to do, you do it.

Laying Down Your Life

Now listen to this. If your wife or children have to worry about the finances of the home—whether you will be broke and lose the house—or if they have to do without the necessities and some pleasures of life, you are not fully doing your job as a father. I mean no condemnation or guilt in that; I just want to motivate you because I know what the end can be. You see, when you do not take on that responsibility, your children have a hard time trusting you—which is the essence of building a relationship. They will also have a hard time trusting God.

Most of the time, they will grow up resenting you and what you put them through. In the meantime, rather than living the life of security that you are to provide, they live a life of anxiety, nervousness and fear. If the home isn't secure, they will not be secure in the world. They will grow up full of fear, worry, and anxieties.

Understand that I am not saying that more income leads to better fathering. The level of income is not as important as a steady income that meets the needs of the family.

Let me explain what I mean. I now realize that growing up, we were poor. I never knew it at the time but looking back, I can see we were poor. I already told you about the year I got a Green Bay Packers trash can and that it was one of the best gifts I ever got. I used it to play basketball, smash-up derby with my cars, as a hockey goal, for marble wars, and for putting golf balls. I used it to toss cards into it, and I even used it for rodeo with the cat. (We would put the cat under it and shake it up. Then we would release the cat, catch it, tie it up—gently, you understand—and throw our hands in the air.) What a great gift!

When I was a kid, I wore secondhand clothes, and my shoes cost only $2. Thrifty ice cream cones were a huge treat, because ten cents for one scoop was a lot of money. I always dreamed of getting a double scoop one day. (Finally, when I was thirty years old, I bought my own triple scoop!) Going out to eat at McDonald's was a real treat that we may have enjoyed once a month. And once in awhile, I got a Happy Meal. All of my toys, besides those I got with the Happy Meals, consisted of thirty match-box cars that I purchased with my own allowance and one Six Million Dollar Man (and, of course, my awesome trash can). Many days, I played outside with a spoon and a couple of cars. My $15 bike was once stolen and then actually brought back (true story). It was easier to carry that bike than it was to pedal it. It seemed to be stuck in tenth gear no matter what you did.

My father didn't make the big bucks but he did bring a steady income, proving that the level of income doesn't make you a better father. Besides, I always knew we would have a roof over our heads, food on the table and gifts at Christmas and birthdays. Maybe they weren't big gifts but we would have gifts. Maybe we wouldn't have the most expensive clothes but we had nice clothes.

A child can't trust a father who doesn't carry the responsibility for the financial welfare of the family. I don't know about you but my kids have enough to worry about in life. And my wife has enough on her plate doing laundry (and, contrary to a couple of humorous comments earlier in the book, she does wash our clothes), getting new clothes for the kids, helping with homework, attending parent-teacher conferences, shopping for groceries, cooking dinner, cleaning house and, of course, tending to me. She doesn't need the worry of finances; I will carry that for the family.

My father didn't make the big bucks but he did bring a steady income.

DAD

Growing up, I knew Dad was the one making it happen for us financially, and I knew he would never let the family fail. You can't put a price tag on what that does to the heart of your children. I am so proud of what my dad did for the family. He laid down his life for us. I read a great book that said, "Greater love has no one than this, than to lay down one's life for his friends."

"Well, Scot, this is all I can earn right now, so we might lose the house. And we'll have no Christmas this year because things are so tight."

That just isn't the right attitude to have. Sure, those may be the circumstances but it still shouldn't be your attitude. You should be speaking life into your kids. You should be speaking security concerning the finances. Never speak what you feel; speak what you believe.

Growing up, when my family first moved out to Arizona, my dad took a job making $4 an hour. Even in 1977, you could not support a family working forty hours a week at $4 an hour. My dad left the house at three in the morning six days a week, and he did not get home until six at night. He was tired but he still found it within himself to spend an hour with my brother Jason and me, put us in bed, spend some time with Mom, and then go out and sell and install smoke detectors until 10 o'clock. He taught Sunday School every week, and some weeks after church, he went out and worked eight more hours.

He worked ninety-plus hours a week and not just for a time but for four or five years.

When my dad came down with mononucleosis, the doctor said he couldn't work, that he had to take a few weeks off. But there was no sick pay at his job. My father knew we couldn't afford that, so he cut back to seventy hours a week so he could rest. Anybody who has had mono knows it takes everything in you just to move, because you're exhausted.

My point is that my father did whatever it took to provide for his family. He felt it was his responsibility. And I'm talking about it from a child's perspective, about the trust and respect that his hard work placed in my heart. My dad laid down his life for me and my brother and mother. What greater act of love could he have done for us? Similarly, we as fathers are called to lay down our own lives for our families.

"Scot, I got laid off, and there are no jobs out there." That's an excuse not to take on your responsibility to your family. And I'm telling you right now, the end result will be children who have no respect for you.

I can remember when my father got laid off. I was in eighth grade. My dad came home and sat the family down and began to tell us about the layoffs. I remember for just a brief second, a little fear came over me about what we would do. For just a second, I wondered, What will happen? Will we lose the house or the car?

My dad was probably scared to death, but with confidence and love in his voice, he said, "It's no big deal. I will make sure everything is fine. Now let's go out to eat."

He didn't talk about cutting back, spending less or not having Christmas or school clothes. He said that Dad would provide. He spoke security into the home and into my heart. During the next eight months of unemployment, I didn't worry one time.

In my heart I said, Dad, I will worry if you say so, and I will be afraid if you want me to. But Dad had conveyed to me that worrying wasn't my job. I was just to let Dad take care of the money. Although there were no jobs for eight months, he worked every odd job he could get his hands on. He sold cars and he did whatever he had to.

I learned in those eight months that Dad would always be there and that I could trust Dad with anything. When you lay down your life like that for your kids, you're teaching them the priceless lesson of trust.

One of the greatest things you can give your children is financial security so that they know Dad will do whatever it takes to provide for and to protect them.

DAD

I want you to know, too, that during the time my father was working all those hours, my mother didn't work. She had a nursing degree and could have made more money than he did, but it was his desire and hers that she remain at home with her children. Can you understand what that put into my heart as a child? Can you sense the pride in my heart about my dad because he provided for the family?

Bear the Burden for Your Family

As I said, your wife should not bear the stress and burden for the family finances. That's why I feel very strongly that men should do the bills and handle the finances. It's not because women can't do it, because they can, and, most the time, they can do a better job.

I feel that men should take care of the finances because women do not need that stress or burden. "Do we have enough money in the bank to cover our outstanding checks? Can we afford a vacation? We need to cut back and do this or that." This could be your wife talking—the one who already has fifty million things to deal with. Now, on top of everything else, she has the concern of the finances. And then you might wonder why she goes off about the littlest things, why she is moody and irritable. It's because she's taking on responsibility that is not hers to take.

~
But Dad had conveyed to me that worrying wasn't my job.
~

Whoever does the bills carries the responsibility for the finances. Even if you work and she stays at home, you should take care of paying the bills and handling the family finances. Sure, you work; you have the job. But if she does the bills, she carries the weight.

Let me give you an analogy to show you what I mean. A few years back, we were having a big party at the house. On this particular day, Holly had an emergency she had to take care of and was gone all day. Now she and I both realize that getting the inside of the house ready for the party was her job, and the outside was mine. She did have the house clean when she left. But I was left with the house. Although it was her responsibility, who was stressed out about the kids making a mess and something getting dirty? I was. Although she usually took care of it, I bore the burden and stress.

The same goes for the bills. Sure, you put the money into the account; you earned the income. But if she is left to handle all the finances, she becomes the one stressed out about whether it will get "dirty" or not.

So take care of those bills. That way, you know when to cut back a little or when you need to get a second job. That should not be her decision to have to make.

My wife has never had a clue about what is in our bank account. And there were times when funds were really low. But she didn't have a clue things were that tight. I had to do some odd jobs to get it turned around but I would not allow her to bear that stress or emotional weight. It's not hers to bear. But had she been doing the bills, she would have had that stress.

"But, Scot, I'm not good at the bills. My wife is much better, and I'm afraid I will screw the finances up. I'm not good with money."

I have an idea to help you become good with money. Suppose your new TV came and you got a new remote control that you've never used before. Do you say, "Well, I'm not good at using this remote. Honey, you learn it, and I'll let you change the channels." No, you don't say that! You'd spend hours programming and learning that thing so you can be good at it.

Similarly, if you're not good with the bills, then get good. "Well, I just can't control my spend-ing." Here's an idea that will help you have a great life, develop self-control, and take on your responsibility as head of the home. Learn addition and subtraction because that's all you really have to know to take care of your family's finances!

Don't give a lame excuse so you can abandon your responsibility. Taking care of the bills is a matter of addition and subtraction! But maybe the reason you make excuses is that deep down, you just don't want that responsibility. It's easier for you to ignore reality than deal with it. It is easier to put money in the bank and not worry about bills getting paid. Great plan, Einstein! Let the love of your life deal with it instead and then wonder why she is so inattentive to you and why she is moody, crabby and stressed out.

I encourage you today that if you're not already doing so to go to your wife and say, "Honey, I want to take on my role as a husband, father and provider. From now on, I will take care of the bills. I will not stress you or the family out. I will bring security to you instead."

And if you're a wife reading this who has been handling your family's finances, learn to give up control of the finances to him. I know you may not want to but you need to trust him and show your kids you trust him.

I'm not saying that you should just spend as much as you and your wife want. But it is your job to make a fair budget for the family spending, making sure that Christmas, birthdays and vacations are well provided for.

I am not saying that you have to do this. But I am saying that if you don't, you are sowing seeds of resentment, and someday you will reap a harvest.

And now that we're on the subject, don't get me started (too late) on men who are behind on their child support or who don't pay at all. You are sabotaging all your hard work at being a great dad. And in the process, you are undermining your children's trust in you. In my book, you are worse than a thief, because most thieves won't steal from family. But if you don't pay child support, you are stealing from your family.

Why do you even owe back child support? "Times were hard, Scot." You can do all the great things with your kids you want, but if Mom is struggling because you aren't providing, you will reap a harvest of resentment one day in the hearts of your children. And your children will go without. Your ex still has to come up with that money. She has to make up for what is lacking from you. She doesn't have the option of "just not having the money, just not feeding the kids, just not clothing the children," because she has a job to do and that is to take care of her children. So what makes you think you as a father should have that option?

Real men, real fathers shouldn't need a court to tell them they're responsible for providing for their children. Real men should be doing much more than what the courts say, anyway. You can't raise a kid on $250 a month. "Hey, I pay what the court says." No, you should be paying what it takes to raise them if you're taking on your responsibility as provider and protector.

To be a great father, you must first achieve the second level of fathering—provider and protector. Dads who do not do this build relationships that will crumble around them one day. You have to work hard to provide

~
Real fathers shouldn't need a court to tell them they're responsible for providing for their children.
~

for your home and family. I promise you dads, if you sow—in this case, into your family—you will reap a harvest of a fulfilled wife and children who take pride in the father who lays down his life to provide for and protect them. And that's priceless!

CHAPTER 17

I WILL BE GOING TO SCHOOL WITH YOU TODAY

This story is an account as told to me by one of
my kids' favorite Sunday School teachers, Miss
Penny. My two oldest children, Laken and Heath, are
at the time six and five years old, respectively. Both
are being brought up in a good, godly home with parents who give their all to place God's values and His
character into their little souls. To fully grasp the fun
of this event, you must know that I am the associate
pastor of my father's church of about 6,000 people.
I teach the parenting class, from which more than
4,000 parents have graduated over the years. People
watch me and my children closely to see if we live
what we preach.

It is a beautiful Sunday morning. My two sons
have just finished up their Bible time. Church is just
getting out, and the children are playing with the toys
as parents begin lining up at the door to pick up their
blessings. Little children—children who are looking to
my children for some guidance and direction—are playing all around the room. Miss Penny is talking to Heath
on one side of the room, while Laken is on the other

side playing with LEGOS (or LOGOS, as my dad calls them). Laken screams across the room, "Miss Penny, look at the ship I made!"

Heath's expression turns to immediate surprise, and he screams out, "Miss Penny, Laken just said SH@#!" (He said the actual word.) He said it so loudly that Miss Penny and all the parents standing around clapped their hands over their mouths and said, "O my gosh!"

In defiance, Laken screams back at Heath, "Liar! I didn't say SH@#—I said ship!"

Heath screams back, "You did not! You said SH@#!"

Miss Penny is frantically trying to stop them. Laken screams again in front of all the parents and all those small, impressionable children, "I said ship, ship, ship—not SH@#!!!"

Heath, to the amazement of all, says in a calm, cool tone: "BULL SH@#!"

Listen to this extreme example, but a great example. What would you do if a man came up and grabbed your-three-year old son from you? What would you do if some man came and snatched your four-year-old daughter out of your hands? Catch them and beat them within an inch of their life. Right? When those words are spoken, anger rises up in you. A sense of protection rises up in you. You will lay down your life at that moment to protect your child. This is the attitude you must have for the rest of your life!

Take that same parent. Where does that instinct of protection go when he finds out his fifteen-year-old daughter is dating some twenty-three-year-old loser. "Well, we tried grounding her. Nothing seems work. So we just hope things turn out well." Heck no! Just like that guy that tried to grab my three-year-old, I will still do whatever it takes. I will lay down my life to save hers! I will put bars on the windows, sleep in her room, go to school with her. I will spend every waking moment of my life guarding my little princess.

Where is that instinct when the father finds out his fourteen-year-old son is hanging out with the wrong crowd? "We tried to get him to stop hanging out with them. Nothing works." What works is your son has no friends. You become his only friend. If I have to, I will go to school with you, be in all your classes. We will have so much fun together. I am willing to lay down my life for you, even give up the love you have for me if that is what it takes.

Believe it or not, there was a season in my life as a young man when I was as convinced of myself—of my superior wisdom and knowledge—as Heath had been that Laken had cursed in church (which both he and Heath

A sense of protection rises up in you. You will lay down your life at that moment to protect your child.

actually did, when all was said and done). At fifteen years of age, I knew it all. For whatever reason, God had blessed me with wisdom far beyond what my parents could even imagine.

I remember sitting on the couch one time, waiting for my dad to come in and give me a little talking to about something I did wrong. My attitude was like, Whatever. What can Dad do? I'm an adult now. So what if I was hanging out with the friend he warned me three times not hang out with and then finally told me I couldn't even talk to. I'm fifteen years old—I can make up my own mind about who to hang out with and who not to.

Just then, Dad walked into the room. Immediately, I noticed he had the "look"—the one that makes me shiver even today. I honestly believe you could do a horror movie called, "The Look" of my dad just staring at you. It would scare the pants off you! My heart skipped a beat, and The Look sucked some of the confidence right out of my body. But I told myself, What's he going to do, ground me? No big deal.

Dad said, "Son, I told you not to hang out with Mike."

"But Dad," I protested, "Mike needs a friend like me to help keep him tuned in to God." (We all know that this excuse is a bunch of baloney.)

"Son," he said, "I don't care about Mike; I care about you. And if you continue to hang out with him, you will find yourself in a lot of trouble in life. So to make sure this never happens again, you will be getting a spanking."

I looked at him and said, "What? I'm fifteen years old! You don't spank a fifteen year-old!"

He said calmly, "Today I do. And you will be grounded until I feel you can make good choices. As of today, you have only one friend, and I am he. At church (this is where Mike and I hung out), you will be at my side the entire time. You will walk with me, go to service with me, go to the bathroom with me. For now, I am all you have."

That day was a turning point in my life. At a time when many teenagers make decisions that ruin their lives or at least destroy a good part of it, my dad said, "No, I love you too much to allow you to do that." Too many dads don't take on the disciplinary role in the family. We want to be the good guy, the "good cop," the friend. Sure, friendship is our ultimate goal, but if you step into that role too early, your child suffers, and in many cases will resent your lack of authority at a time in his life when he needed it most.

Instead, I am so grateful that my father took on his role. Sure, at the time, I was mad and upset. But great fathers don't care as much about the moment as we care about the end result.

When I was in twelfth grade, the school was having trouble with me not attending classes. My dad found out and sat down with me to talk. Once again, I'm confident, thinking, What are you going to do, Pop?

He said, "Son, if you cut class one more time, I will have to take vacation from work. And then what I will do is go to school with you each day. Once again, I will be your best friend. We will sit in class together. I will go to lunch with you and hang out at the lockers with you. We will spend all day every day together until I feel I can trust you to go to class."

Well, there was no way I was going to hang out with Dad at school, so I didn't miss another class!

Your children have to know that you will do whatever it takes to help them make good choices in life. I can't tell you how many times as a pastor I have had dads in my office telling me they have no control over their teenage son or daughter. "My daughter sneaks out every night," one dad told me. Well, then my advice is that she will be sleeping in her parents' room every night until she stops sneaking out. "Well, she's fifteen and dating this guy, and I can't stop it." Yes, you can. You can do whatever it takes to protect your children from making life-destroying decisions.

As a teenager, my brother was dating a girl who was all trouble. Jason was fifteen years old and my parents found out she had sent him pictures of her wearing a nightie. They told him he couldn't go see her or talk to her. Like me, Jason put up an initial fight, which had similar results as mine. But the girl kept calling and writing letters. So my dad took her dad out and told him that his daughter was a slut (I'm sorry about using that word, but that is the strength of the tone Dad felt he needed to convey to get the result he wanted). You can guess what happened; that relationship quickly ended.

Up until the time your kids are out of the house, you are responsible for the decisions they make.

You Can Get Involved!

Many parents sit back and say, "There's nothing we can do." We tried grounding him, but he sneaks out. We said no, but he did it, anyway. But, you know, my brother could have easily become a father at fifteen years old. My parents said, "Your future is so important to us that we will make sure you don't make a horrible decision."

You have to ask yourself, what is your child's future worth? Up until the time your kids are out of the house, you are responsible for the decisions they make. Your fourteen-year-old daughter is dating a nineteen-year-old guy. That's your fault, and if you don't take care of it, your daughter will be setting her future up for disaster.

You have to have the mindset that you will do whatever it takes to change your kids' direction when they're headed down the wrong path. Wrong friends can destroy their lives, so until they show you that they can pick the right friends, it might be up to you to pick their friends. A wrong girlfriend can destroy your son's life. Obviously, if he can't pick the right girl, Dad will pick for him (this sounds like a fifteenth-century type of arranged marriage, but you know what I mean). If kids don't want to go to school, Dad can fix that. Dad will steer the kids' lives until they learn to steer them themselves. I'm not saying you should do this in an over-controlling way. Just don't let your kids walk down a destructive path. You have the power to stop them from hurting themselves.

Later in life, your child will say, as I did, "Thanks, Dad." When my dad took me aside like that, I can't tell you how much trust that built inside me. He put up with my being mad and upset because he loved me enough to discipline me. He loved me enough to say no. In that, it built respect and trust inside me.

You have to be your child's moral conscience until your child can make the right choices on his or her own. What that means is, you make their decisions until they are at a point in life when they can make right decisions.

I have parents ask me all the time at what age a girl can date. I say, "How do I know? I don't know your daughter." There is no age at which all teenage girls are ready to date. If she's seventeen years old dating a dropout loser with no job, and he treats her like garbage, guess what? She isn't old enough to date.

I had a father one night show up at a men's meeting talking about how his fourteen-year-old daughter ran away the day before and how he and his wife decided that they wouldn't allow this to affect their lives. I told him, "You go get in the car, search the streets and go to the boyfriend's house and scare the living heck out of him."

"Yeah," her father said, "but she will just run away again." I said, "That would be very hard to do with her father right by her side all the time. I tell you what. You go to school with her and to class with her. You have lunch together. You wait outside the stall in the women's bathroom if you have to. Let her know that you love her so much, you will lay down your life so she doesn't end up losing hers."

Dads have said, "But I can't get her to stop dating this bum." I guarantee I could! "I can't get my son to go to school." I guarantee I could! "I can't get my son to hang out with the right friends." I guarantee I could! Why am I so confident? Because I know that I would lay my life down so that my children wouldn't lose theirs.

But many dads today give up their children's future because they give up on the moment. They have this attitude of just giving up and leaving their kids' futures to whatever happens.

You have to be able to say, "Can't pick out right music? Guess what—I will pick it." "Can't be responsible with how much TV you watch? Guess what—I will show you how." "Failing your classes? Guess what—I will call the teacher every day, get the assignment for the night, and sit beside you while you do your homework. We will check it and go over it until it is perfect. I will know when your tests are, and I will teach you how to study. And until you can get good grades on your own, Dad will be right there to make sure you do."

Until your children have the mental capacity to make right choices, it is your responsibility to make the choices for them—end of story.

That is the heart and attitude of a great father. Anything less, and the rest of this book can be used to clean up the dog's mess. You see, all kids test the water, but if Dad isn't willing to dive in to save his son or daughter from drowning, what does anything else he has done matter?

Your children may hate it at the time, but if you don't discipline them, down the road they may resent you for allowing them to ruin their lives!

Learn How To Discipline Rightly

I feel it's important that you learn how to properly discipline in love. This book is not about that, so go out and get other books that specifically deal with discipline. Find out the right ways to discipline in love.

For you to read this chapter and then just start spanking your kids is not my intention, and it will do more damage than good. I believe that to randomly spank or discipline without any training is more damaging than not disciplining at all. It's like throwing an eight-year-old behind the wheel of a Diesel and saying, "Drive!" He will do more damage than good.

You can't just go into the programming files of your computer and type in random things. You will mess it up. You have to learn the codes, when to do things and when not to. It's the same thing with your kids. There are plenty of books, tapes, and other material on raising kids. Get hold of some of them and learn how to discipline rightly.

This knowledge will give you confidence. You see, when I know that what I'm doing is right, I can step out into disciplining my children more confidently. But if I'm not sure—if I think, Maybe it is right, maybe it's not—it keeps me from stepping out. Or they try something half way, didn't really work, so they give up. Now they try something else. Most of the time it doesn't work

> You can't just go into the programming files of your computer and type in random things.

because you're not committed to it. Kids are smart. They know they just have to wait out the new discipline fad. If I pout long enough, throw a big enough fit, my parents will give up. Why do they give up? Because they lack confidence in it. Many parents do nothing because they have no confidence. And who ends up suffering? The child whose parents gave him no direction or structure.

Kids who have direction, structure, and discipline in their lives are a lot happier than kids who do not. How would you like to work at a job where you never knew what was expected of you? Some days you got in trouble for one thing, but the next day, you didn't get in trouble for something you did that was even worse. And then some days, if the boss was moody, you got in trouble for nothing at all. It would be a very confusing, annoying world.

Kids are the same; they are happier when they know what to expect. Kids whose parents go off on them on every whim of emotion—sometimes they get in trouble for this; at other times, they don't—experience a very confusing world. The real problem with this is that kids are gamblers at heart. They think that if they get into trouble only one out of three times for something, more than likely, they will try it again.

I said all that to say this. Learn how to discipline your kids with consistency. Get into some classes and get some books if you need to. A great proverb says, "Train up a child in the way he should go, and when he is old he will not depart from it." You see, it is your job to train them up through proper, consistent discipline.

In all this, remember that the goal of discipline is to change direction. If my child is headed down a wrong road, how do I change his or her direction? Each child is a little different. For some kids, taking away the phone and TV will change their direction. Others may need a more strict approach.

Dad Is the Disciplinarian

You have to be the primary source of discipline in the home. You should make Mom out to be the "good cop," and you should take on the role of "bad cop." You should make sure that the kids are more afraid of coming against Mom than even you. Make sure the kids honor and lift up Mom.

Don't ever say things like, "Your mom wants you grounded. I tried to talk her out of it, but she wants it." No, you say, "Mom really wants me to lessen the punishment, but your mistake is huge, and I have to treat it huge. (To me, it doesn't even matter if that's true or not. In our family, I always take on the role of "bad cop.")

"But, Scot, that's not right! Why should I be the bad guy all the time?" Because it is right, and we have to get to the place where we want what's right for the kids, not for us. We want the kids to esteem Mom and lift her up. I guarantee if you do this, you will put so much respect and trust in your child's heart. Even today, I have a high level of reverence toward my mom, and I have a huge respect toward my dad. If I can trust Dad to look out for Mom, the woman he says he loves, I know I can trust Dad to look out for me.

The bottom line is that sometimes you have to take a hard stand on an issue if your child is walking down a dangerous path, headed to destruction. Get involved in steering your children in the right direction! Just remember that discipline must always be consistent and practiced in love. Your being the disciplinarian of your home is ultimately a wonderful way to earn respect and trust in your relationship with your children. And, really, it may just save their lives.

CHAPTER 18

BECOMING COACH LOMBARDI

Last year, I was one of the coaches for Laken's baseball team. During one particular game, we're at the bottom of the last inning with one out. Laken is the winning run on first base. I'm the first-base coach. I'm the one who's going to tell him what to do: steal, stay, hold up, lead off, and so forth. But all around us are hundreds of parents, players, and other coaches all trying to add their input as to what Laken should do: "LEAD OFF, LAKEN!" "STEAL, LAKEN!" "GO! RUN, LAKEN!!!"

But in the middle of all these voices, he hears Dad say, "Listen to me, Son. I will tell you what to do."

Now, Laken and his teammates are still at the age at which kids don't fully grasp the "if-the-pop-fly-is-caught-you-have-to-stay-on-base" rule. Crack! One of our players hits a powerhouse hit. Laken starts to run, and the crowd is screaming, "RUN, LAKEN, RUN!" And Laken is running.

I scream, "Laken! Stop!" And in the middle of all the noise and confusion of hearing fifty other instructions coming at him from every direction, Laken is able to pull my voice out from all the other voices and follow my instructions. He stops. The ball is caught, but Laken gets back to first, and later that inning, he scores.

When your child becomes a teenager, there will be so many voices in his or her life screaming out instructions. Try drugs, try sex, ditch school, let's smoke, let's sneak out… In the midst of all these other voices, I want my children to be able to hear my voice and to follow my instructions as the coach of their lives.

In sports today, we are finding out that the success of a team has more to do with the coach of the team than the talent of the team. Take Bill Parcells, for instance, the coach of the Dallas Cowboys. He took a last-place team and, without changing much of the roster, took them to the playoffs the first year he coached them. It was the same talent as before, but a different coach.

As a dad, you are the coach of the team, and that team is your family. The success or failure of the team is your responsibility, with, of course, the help of your co-coach, your wife. But I always put more responsibility on myself if the team fails and give more credit to my wife if it succeeds.

Now, you may think that's not fair. Well, it's not fair that when a sports team loses and there are plenty of people to blame, the coach is the only one who gets fired. Yet when the team does well, a great coach gives the credit to all those around him.

So it is with fathers. A family that is falling apart is his responsibility, and a successful family is successful because of all those around him.

A great coach has the trust of those on his team. His team believes in him and in what he is doing for them. The team believes that the coach has their interests in mind. As fathers, this is our job. Our wife and children should know that our decisions are best for them and not just for ourselves. They should be able to trust in us and believe in us. They should know that we are taking them toward success.

Here are some things you can do as the coach to ensure a winning team—a happy and fulfilled family.

Put the Team First

Number one, as I said, your team must know that you have their best interests in mind. As dads, we must display an attitude of laying down our lives for the family and of giving in to their needs instead of our own. Oftentimes, I know after a long, hard day at work, you want to "veg out" in front of the TV. But someone who wants the best for the team will put the team's needs first. So that means you spend the first part of the night with the co-coach, Mom, as I talked about in previous chapters. You then spend time with your kids. You help with homework. You make sure the team helps clean the kitchen.

The success or failure of the team is your responsibility.

You must display the attitude that the team is more valuable in your life than anything else, including yourself. A team that knows the coach has laid down his life for them will lay down their lives for that coach.

Encourage a Sense of Team Identity

The second thing fathers can do as coach is to encourage and develop a sense of teamwork within the family. The successful teams are the ones who work together, who have the mindset, This is our team, and we will stick together no matter what happens. Anytime you get a team with even one player who is all about himself instead of about the team—one player who is "out of there" the first chance he gets—that team will see little success.

Families that, in a sense, all go their own way—families that are made up of "me's" and not "we's"—see little success in relationships within the family. These are the families that later in life bear through holidays, can't stand family gatherings, and only get together because they have to.

As the coach, it is your job to create a team atmosphere. In our family, we are "The Andersons." It's great to be on this team. This team sticks together, we watch out for one another, we never give up, and we never quit.

Being a part of this team is not an option; it is a requirement. God, the great General Manager in the sky, put this roster together and made us a family. I can honestly say to my kids, "Sorry, Son, you're not a free agent until, let me see here—oh yeah, the end of eternity." No, I tell them that from the beginning, they are an Anderson. Andersons love others. Andersons are givers. Andersons respect their elders. Andersons are not doormats that people can walk all over. We stand up for ourselves and for what is right.

As I was growing up, being an Anderson meant we lived by a different standard. At times it felt unfair and made me mad, but underneath all that was pride: I was an Anderson and part of a successful team, an elite team. Why is that special? Think, for example, about the people who go through the grueling hard work of becoming a Navy Seal. Why do they do it? Well, partly because as Seals, they are elite and they are a part of a team that commands honor and dignity.

Let me give you another example of how being a part of a special team affects its players. To play for Vince Lombardi, coach of the Green Bay Packers from 1958-1968, was an honor. The Packers had standards and a code of honor: Packers play when they are hurt. Packers never give up. Packers practice harder than anyone else. Think with me—why wouldn't you want to play for another team, where it is easier, where you can lay back a little? I'll tell you. Because inside of each one of us is a drive for excellence, a drive to be a part of a winning team.

Fathers should use that drive. Sure, it isn't fair, and it is more work to be a member of a winning team, but we are winning the most important game of all—the game of life. Dads are responsible for creating this sense of teamwork among the family.

Tell the Team What You Believe

The third thing you can do as coach is tell the team what you believe. In other words, put in their hearts how you as a family will play the game of life. Tell them what the playbook is that you make your decisions by.

What would happen on a football team if the coach has a playbook for a 3-4 defense but some of the team believe in the 4-6 defense. So they refuse the 3-4, while others don't even have that playbook, because they want to simply play a nickel defense, and still others want a dime defense. Do you see the confusion? That's why it is very important that your whole team is playing with the same "playbook." Each member must have the same beliefs, morals and attitudes toward life.

Holly and I are proud that we are instilling our biblical belief system into our children. We won't wait until they are thirteen years old to sit them down and say, "Here is what we believe. I hope you agree."

As your children grow up, they will have questions about the playbook. They will begin to question the beliefs. But it is important that the coach and co-coach stand strong and say, "This is what we believe, and here is why. This belief will produce a great life for you." (Of course, if you don't have a great life, then you need to get a whole bunch of books and study them to get your beliefs right.)

Growing up, I would say about wanting to do certain things, "But, Dad, all the other kids are doing it."

Dad would say, "That's fine, but we won't do it because we are Andersons. We as a family do not believe in that. We believe strongly that right is right and wrong is wrong, even if everybody else is doing it. We will stick together on our beliefs."

I remember in junior high school how at church all the couples would go to the park behind the church. Of course, they would make out and do whatever else. Finally, I got a girlfriend (after thousands of hours of prayer). That first Sunday night, Lisa and I walked out into the park just holding hands. Realize that we didn't even kiss. We just walked and talked. That night, my father, who was the pastor, got eight calls from people concerning my being in the park. Three of them had kids

~

We won't wait until they are thirteen years old to sit them down and say, "Here is what we believe. I hope you agree."

~

who spent a whole lot of time in the park doing things
I still haven't done! (In fact, one of the gentlemen who
called, Mr. Let-Me-Pick-the-Speck-Out-of-Your-Eye,
became a grandpa a little sooner than he expected.)

I said, "Dad, I didn't do anything!"

He said, "I know, Son, but that's not the point.
Andersons need to abstain from even the appearance of
evil. There's no reason why you and Lisa can't walk
around the parking lot and talk."

"But, Dad," I insisted, "everyone else is doing it."

Dad said, "Everyone else isn't my responsibility;
you are. And you know that we as a family don't believe
in that."

Put that into their hearts and they will give you
theirs.

Fathers, we build attitudes into the lives of each
family member. We shape, mold and influence the morals and actions of our family according to our playbook.
How others look at your family is your responsibility.

Do people say, "Oh, the Andersons are coming
over. Better get ready for the little terrors." Or is it,
"Boy, the Andersons are such a pleasure to have over.
The Andersons are such a great family."?

Lombardi was such an amazing coach that when a
player messed up, the player felt bad for the team, not just
for himself. Coach Lombardi had influenced the players

so that their attitude was, Look at how my mistake affected the team. Lombardi taught them that if each player didn't prepare, it affected the entire team.

CHAPTER 19

I LOVE YOU! NOW GET OUT OF MY FACE

Little Peyton is my two-year-old and is quite possibly the cutest thing in the world. He has blonde, super curly hair and a smile that can melt your heart. If you were to ask me Peyton's favorite place in the world, I wouldn't say Disneyland, LEGOLAND, or even the beach. I would have to say it is our pantry. To Peyton, this enormous place filled with cookies, toaster pastries, cereal bars, chips, candy, and other goodies is heaven. We have a huge walk-in pantry with a glass door that we have to keep closed, or Peyton would weigh 400 pounds. But in the course of any given day, somebody leaves the door open, and into heaven Peyton will go.

You can always tell when Peyton has entered the pantry, because, all of a sudden, you'll hear him scream out, "YEAHHH!!!" as he claps his hands. He does realize that after his scream of excitement, he has only about fifteen seconds to eat all he can.

So here we are just before time to leave for church. Holly is already at the church teaching, which leaves me alone with the children. I'm in the middle of combing my four-year-old's hair when I hear, "YEAH-HH!!!" I stop what I'm doing and go to the pantry. To my surprise, Peyton is scaling the shelves like a skilled mountain climber. He already has in his hands the candy tote and is lowering it to the floor.

I say, "Peyton, no."

He says, "Daddy, nanny." He then looks at me with those huge blue eyes and says, "Pleeeeeze? Just on' (that's one), Daddy?"

I say, "Okay, just one."

I give him one little candy, close the pantry, and go back to combing Baylor's hair. Not two minutes later, I hear, "YEAHHH!!!"

What in the world…, I think as I rush over the pantry again.

Now Peyton is shoveling candy into his mouth. He says, "Mmm, Daddy, mmm."

"No, Peyton. No more candy!"

He then swallows the pound of candy and points his tiny finger at me and says, "No, Daddy, no! On' more nanny!"

I say, "No," and I take the candy tote away from him and remove him from the pantry. In an instant, Peyton goes from happy little son to screaming son.

Now, we don't allow fits in my house, so I put him in the corner, which is really cute to see him cry in the corner, while we laugh at him (that last part about laughing is a joke, but it is cute).

Once again, I try to finish combing Baylor's hair when all of a sudden, I hear the tap, tap, tap of little feet running. Peyton is making a break for the pantry. In amazement, I'm thinking, Do you really think I can't catch you? I put the comb down and start to walk over to the pantry when Peyton closes the door. I'm thinking, What! Do you really think I can't open that door? But then he locks the door from the inside! I now have my face pressed up against the glass watching him clap his hands and scream, "YEAHHH!!!"

I scream out, "Peyton, you open this door!"

He stops clapping, looks at me, and says, "No, Da-Da, no!" He then opens the candy tote and begins to eat.

I say, "No, Peyton!"

He looks at me and says, "Yes, yes!"

I scream out, "PEYTON, YOU OPEN THIS DOOR RIGHT NOW! PUT THAT CANDY DOWN RIGHT NOW! DO YOU HEAR ME!"

To my great amazement, he turns to me, puts his finger to his lips, and goes, "Sshhhhh." (That was funny.)

I scream, "Someone get Daddy a screwdriver—Dad's breaking into the pantry!"

I run to the garage, get a screwdriver, come back in, and begin to pick the lock. Peyton, understanding

In an instant, Peyton goes from happy little son to screaming son.

what is happening, begins to shove all the candy he possibly can into his mouth. He's probably figuring, If I'm going to get a spanking, I will make sure it's worth it.

As you read this chapter, realize that I saved some of the most important things for last. The material contained in this chapter has to do with setting the mood in your home, and I'll just say this. The mood you consistently set in your home will affect, for good or bad, the relationship you will have with your children when they are grown.

Picture the following scenario. Here you are out to lunch with an acquaintance or friend. This made-up scenario is one I would be willing to bet we've all had happen with our kids at home. All of a sudden, in the middle of the meal, your adult friend knocks over a glass of milk that he was drinking.

Now, how do you respond to this person who probably won't be in your life in a few years—this person who doesn't mean half as much to you as your own child? Do you say, "What in the world are you doing? Where is your head? Can you not focus for two minutes? Can't you use two hands on your glass like you're supposed to? Will you look at that—it's all over the place!" (It's funny how we always want our kids to look at it.) "What am I supposed to do?" your rampage continues. "Now I have to clean up your mess, because you can't watch what you're doing! You know what—you're never going to get milk in a glass ever again. From now on, we're just going to put all your drinks in a sippy cup."

Is that how you would respond to your friend or acquaintance—this relatively meaningless person in your life? Probably not. But how do you respond to your child in similar situations? Do you give him or her the same type of respect as this person who in ten years probably won't remember you?

How about a scenario in which you're working at your office, you're busy, and a co-worker comes up to you and says, "Hey, I have a quick question for you."

How do you respond to this co-worker whom you barely even know? Do you say, "Can I not have two or three minutes to myself? I just want to get some things done around here! Can life not be about you all day? Can I have a little peace and quiet for one minute? I'd like to have just three minutes at a time when I could just focus on something I want to focus on. You know what—go to your cubicle and don't you come out till I get done!"

Is that how you would respond to your co-worker? No, of course it isn't. But do you show your children at least the same emotional stability that you would show a person who means nothing to you? Could your children have that much from you?

Now listen to my heart on this. I'm not saying that we're to be our kids' best friends who can never mete out any kind of discipline or a reprimand when it's called for. No, I'm still the parent. I'm still guiding and directing my children, and, hopefully, by the age of nineteen, my goal of friendship will be attained. But how I as a father respond to my children should always be about relationship-building, not about emotional rampaging that tears the relationship down.

The Relationship Should Affect the Response

If you went off like I described earlier on your friend who spilled his milk, would you have any chance at a friendship with him? Probably not. For the same reason you wouldn't berate your friend, you should also change your responses to your kids. If one of my kids is fooling around and spills a glass of milk, I remain calm because I don't want to do anything to hinder the relationship. I reply, "You know what—when you have milk in a glass, you need to watch what you're doing. I want you right now to clean up the milk. And if you can't handle the responsibility of milk in a glass, Dad's going to have to give you a sippy cup until you can."

If I want a relationship with my child, I will just calmly deal with the situation. I won't scream, holler, and yell. I won't look like a lunatic or a nut in front of my child, going off because of a little bit of spilled milk in his life. Most importantly, I won't hurt the relationship over something as meaningless as milk.

If your children keep interrupting you while you work, teach them how to do it correctly. If you teach your children how to interrupt correctly, when they become adults, interrupting other adults will not be annoying to all those around them.

So I taught my kids how to interrupt, and when they do come to talk to me while I'm busy, first, I take a breath and think to myself, My children's needs are very important to me. Then I reply, "Is this an emergency? No? Okay, Dad's in the middle of doing something right now. If you'll give me about twenty or thirty minutes, Dad's going to come help you, and he's going to take care of your problem."

Do you see the difference in the response when relationship is important? I've done it the other way when I've been busy with something frustrating. One of my children would come to me with a question and out of me would come garbage. I had to change, and you may need to change, too.

This chapter is about changing probably the most important area of our lives. If you will change this one area, I believe you will change everything. Again, I'm talking about setting the mood of your home.

I won't hurt the relationship over something as meaningless as milk.

The Mood of the Home Mirrors the Father

When I told my wife that I was going to write that Dad is the one who sets the atmosphere or mood of the home, she said that, no, Mom is the one who sets the mood of the home. This discussion led to a fight, during which I really made her mad, and she proved to me that Mom has the power to set the mood of the home!

However, based on deep conviction and just a little defiance, I will state unswervingly that the mood of the home indeed mirrors the father, not the mother. What emotion you bring to breakfast seems to linger and follow the kids throughout the day. What you bring home from work sets the atmosphere for the night. Have you ever noticed that Mom can be mad and upset, and her mood doesn't really "attach" to us?

For example, Mom can say, "No one cleans up after himself in this house! You guys are a bunch of pigs, and I'm done (why are moms always "done"?) cleaning up after you! I cook, I clean, and no one helps! No one can seem to hit the toilet! Well, I have news for you…" (she always has some news for us, but it's usually yesterday's news—we've already heard it).

Okay, during this mild tantrum (sorry, Honey, if you're reading this part), it's almost funny. I mean, we're respectful. We apologize, and we love on Mom.

Afterward, we go on our way, and like I said, that mood doesn't really attach to us.

But if Dad is ever to say, "I WANT SOME PEACE AND QUIET IN THIS HOUSE NOW!"—suddenly, something different is in the air. The mood and atmosphere changes in the kids and in the home.

I'm not saying that a moody mom doesn't affect the home, but I believe that the father leads the family with his emotion. If your wife is always moody, going off on you and the kids, look first to the attitude you bring into the house. Obviously, I can't generalize, but most of the time, if you will change your attitude, she will follow.

If Dad is happy and excited about the day in the morning and comes home happy and excited about the night, soon the family will be excited about life, too. If Dad is moody and nobody can talk to him in the morning, or if they have to leave Dad alone when he gets home, that home can become a heavy, dark, and uninviting place.

What most dads don't realize is that what they set up in the home is what their kids take into the world and into their future homes. The atmosphere you set can dictate how they see the world, life, and relationships.

Put on a Smile and Make Happiness a Choice

I almost didn't think to talk in this book about what Dad reflects in the home, because moodiness wasn't allowed in my home growing up. As a habit, my parents were not down, depressed or moody. Now, they had plenty of circumstances and excuses to be, yet they weren't. When my dad was working almost 100 hours a week just to keep food on the table, he would have had a reasonable excuse to be tired, irritable and moody. But he wasn't.

When my dad got laid off for eight months, that could have been a perfect excuse to be depressed and think, Poor me! Life isn't fair, and I think I'm going to have a mid-life crisis. But he didn't. After that my dad suffered a heart-attack. He could have said, "Poor me, nothing ever goes my way. I'm going to buy a corvette and get me an eighteen-year-old girlfriend." After that, Dad basically got reamed over as an associate pastor of a church where he laid down his life. They sent him out to fail in some small-town church that they planned on taking away from him in a month, so that way, there would be no ripples in the congregation. It could have been the perfect time for him to be mad at God and life. But he wasn't. No matter what happened in life, my dad demonstrated that happiness is a choice.

We will always have problems in life, but how you deal with them dictates how successful and great your life will be. I now carry over into my life the heritage my father gave me. Every day of life is great! I have an amazing, happy, joy-filled life. Though I have big problems just like everyone else, I know that problems don't have to dictate my mood and that other people can't make me feel something; I dictate my mood.

Few people have had as bad a childhood as my mother. Her childhood was filled with physical and emotional abuse and abandonment. Yet in my home growing up, we didn't allow ourselves to be crabby, depressed or unhappy. So as a child, I never knew she'd had those problems.

I hear of homes in which the family knows not to talk to Dad in the morning. He just isn't a morning person. Then when Dad gets home, the family knows to leave him alone until after dinner. And the kids walk around on eggshells, so to speak, because Mom is stuck in her depression and might go off at any time.

> I know that problems don't have to dictate my mood and that other people can't make me feel something.

Whose Image Are You Reflecting?

As a dad, it is your job to be the head of the home. And as the spiritual head, it should be your goal to guide and direct the entire family in the direction of having the right home atmosphere. And what kind of home is that? It is a home that is full of love, joy, peace and kindness.

A home environment as intended, is one in which something is different when someone steps into your home. Yours is a home where happiness reigns in the home—if one of your children's friends come over any time of any day, he should be able to say to you, "Something's different about this house. How come this house is so different? How come this house is so happy? How come when you ask your kids to do something, they do it without throwing a fit and slamming doors. What is different about this house?"

It is your responsibility as a father to get up every day with the attitude, This is a great day! Circumstances will not direct my day. Instead, I direct my day. I show my day how I'm supposed to feel. And as I begin to interact with my kids, I teach them, too, that circumstances don't dictate or direct our emotions.

It is interesting that in life you almost always get what you expect. If you expect a bad day, you get a bad day. But if you expect a great day, you always get a great day. In my life, I have never had a bad day. Sure I had some negative circumstances, but at the end of the day, all the great in my life outweighs the bad. If at the end of the day I have my beautiful wife and four boys, what else do I need?

Every day you should get up and expect a great day. This is what you should demonstrate to your children. Moodiness and crabbiness should not be allowed in your home. Teach your children to put a smile on their face when they come to breakfast. The rule should be, "If you're not happy, then go back to your room. When you can be happy, come on out, because we are one happy family!"

Laken is six and is learning to ride his new scooter. Being quite athletic, he picks up the skill right away. But Laken, wanting to always push the limits, wants to also do wheelies like Dad. Now going up the hill is no problem, but going down the hill seems to pose a big problem. He can't do it! By the third time, this child who has been raised by a pastor begins to show Daddy's patience. He throws his scooter down and yells, "I HATE THIS STUPID DUMB SCOOTER. I WISH IT WOULD BREAK. I HATE MY LEGS, I...I...JUST WANT TO BE A BABY LIKE BAYLOR SO I NEVER HAVE TO RIDE THIS DUMB THING!!!"

I say "Laken, we don't talk like that. Just keep trying and you will get it, but getting mad does no good." (He's probably thinking, Ditto, Dad when you're working on the car.)

So Laken tries again, same scenario. "I HATE THIS STUPID THING. IT'S DUMB, DUMB, DUMB. I WISH I WAS GOD BECAUSE I WOULD BREAK THIS THING!!!"

I say "Laken that is enough. We are out here to have fun, and we will have fun. You will be happy. I don't want to hear any of that garbage come out of your mouth again. When you get down the hill you will have a smile on your face and say, 'I love this scooter,' or you will find yourself in a whole lot of trouble. Do you understand me!"

"Yes, Dad," he says in a monotone voice.

I then began to pray. And in my mind, I'm not asking for a lot. I mean, we have turned water into wine, parted the Red Sea, raised Lazarus. We can surely let the child do a wheelie. But God didn't feel like a miracle was needed in this situation.

So of course Laken fails to do a wheelie. He turned bright red. You could see the anger on his face. He was so mad he could barely breathe. He goes to throw his scooter, stops in the middle. He puts on the most forced smile ever and, in a sarcastic voice, says, "Whoopie, whooptie do. I love this stupid, stupid, stupid scooter. It's so much stupid fun I can't stand it." Then he walks up the hill.

In the mornings growing up, I might not have had a good night. The day might not have been all it should be. But when you came out to breakfast at the Anderson's house you put on a smile like Dad's. You said good morning and acted happy. Funny thing is, no matter how I felt when I got up, by the time break-fast was over, I honestly could say, "This is going to be a great day."

It is a father's job to train his children and lead his family in the direction of a happy home atmosphere. He is to train his children not to talk back to Mom—not to sass her, because "we're not cranky in this home. We don't do those things." This home isn't moody, isn't depressed. This home is up and happy.

Dad is to train his children and demonstrate to them what the correct attitude of the home should be. And as he begins to change the attitude of the home, he begins to change the attitude his kids will take out into the world. They will no longer take the moodiness and other junk with them out into the world. Instead, they are a bright light of great emotions that shines forth into the lives of others.

It is Dad's responsibility to set the mood of hap-piness in his home every day. How sad is it for a child to learn before he goes off to school that he can't talk to his dad? His dad's in the newspaper or busy watching ESPN in the morning. The child then goes off into the world thinking maybe the world will answer some of his ques-tions—maybe the world will be there for him. The child will hope that the world can give him some sort of secu-rity, because he can't get it at home.

~

Dad is to train his children and demonstrate to them what the correct attitude of the home should be.

~

You know, when Dad gets home from work, his children have missed him all day, but how often do they know to keep away from him because he's going to be cranky from the stress of work and the traffic coming home. He has to go off by himself and watch TV for a few hours while the rest of the family keeps quiet. How sad is it that kids can't get excited about seeing Dad come home and being able to share their day with him and have him share his with them?

At Your House, Is It All About You?

When kids have to walk around the house on eggshells because Dad's deep in depression, something is wrong in that house. Everything has to be quiet and perfect or Dad will go off on them. All of sudden, the kids are trying to figure out how they can fix Dad's world—how they can make Dad happy. And so they're doing this, that and the other thing, trying to make Dad happy.

Kids have enough to worry about without worrying about fixing your life. They should be focused on getting their lives in order!

There are dads out there who will steal their kid's money to buy booze and drugs. These dads will sell their kid's PlayStations® or Xboxes™ to get drugs. As horrible as that sounds, do you want to know what I feel is worse? A parent who steals his child's joy. I really do feel it's worse. It takes a very self-centered person to steal their kid's PlayStation® or bike. We probably all could agree on that. But what kind of person would steal their child's joy and happiness?

"Well, you don't understand. I'm depressed," you might say. So that gives you a right to steal your kid's joy?

Actually, depression is simply about self. (This might make some people mad, but they are probably the ones who are already given to anger and self-centeredness.) Now, obviously, some depression is clinical and requires medical attention, but I'm talking about the selfish kind of depression that is consumed with "my past, my circumstances, my stress, my anxieties, my heartache, my pain, my life!" Furthermore, these people have the attitude, So, because of how I feel, I will make everyone around me feel miserable. I have no joy and happiness, so I will steal theirs. I have my moodiness, my stress on the job and my things to worry about. Therefore, I will put all of these things on my children and rob them of their joy and happiness in their home life. That is my right.

But you never, ever have the right to steal a child's happiness, to take away his joy or peace. You never have a right to exalt your problems and emotions as more important than anyone else's, as if to say, "My problems and emotions are more important than yours. So I will pull you down and make you feel bad because I feel bad. What you're feeling doesn't matter; what matters is how I feel."

The Memory Kids Take With Them Will Determine the Relationship You'll Have With Them

I'm not saying that, as dads, we are never to make a single mistake. Remember, it's how we're characterized overall that counts. I know in my own life, there will still be a day now and then when I'm feeling a little stressed. I'm still going to have days when things don't go well at work. Growing up, my dad may have had a bad day or two—but, you see, I can't remember them, because my dad was characterized as being a great dad every day. He was characterized in my childhood as being happy. And so in my lifetime, all I can remember is that my house—my home life—was happy. As I said, moodiness was never a part of my home. We were not allowed to be moody and unhappy at our house.

Let's not Kill Heath Today!

Baylor, my four-year-old calls it "Me and Dad Time." He absolutely loves "Me and Dad Time," a time of just he and I doing something together. We may go get a Slushy, play basketball, or play some other game. But whatever it is, it is time spent together, just the two of us.

And so it's "Me and Baylor Time," and we're sitting at the kitchen table coloring. Laken has a friend over, and it's about eight o'clock at night. They had asked if they could go outside to eat their popsicles. All of a sudden, they come running in the door.

Slam! Laken and his friend have this exaggerated expression of fake terror, and they have their hands across the door as if they're going to protect us from impending danger. Laken's friend cries out, "He's trying to kill us!" Now, Laken and his friend were playing a little pretend game of "the bad guy is outside trying to get us." I know this, you know this, but Baylor doesn't know this.

Laken's friend says again, "He's trying to kill us right now."

I say, "Boys, we don't talk like that."

Then, as if to play along with them somewhat, I say, "All right, guys, go downstairs and play, and everything will be fine." So they go downstairs and I don't think anything more about it.

Baylor and I continue coloring, and Heath comes into the kitchen. Understand that although Heath and Baylor are very good friends, Heath tends to tease Baylor a little bit—actually, quite a bit. Heath comes over and

~

In my lifetime, all I can remember is that my house— my home life— was happy.

~

is peeking over Baylor's shoulders, grabbing his crayons and just being annoying. I say, "Heath, we don't do mean things to our brother. I need you to go find something to do. It's 'Me and Baylor Time' right now."

Heath says, "Dad can I go outside and get my truck?"

"Yes, Son."

Just as Heath was about to open the door, Baylor looks up, and I could see the fear on his face. He cries out, "HEATH, YOU CAN'T GO OUTSIDE! THERE'S A…" (long pause as he thinks for a minute). Then Baylor says, "Never mind" and goes back to his coloring.

Outside Stimuli That Affects the Atmosphere of the Home:

You see, as a dad, doing the things that maintain peace in your home is your responsibility. What your kids see in you, they will do. You need to understand that what is going into your kids will come out of them and will affect their lives. What I allow to be poured into the minds of my children, whether it's through TV, radio, or anything else, will come out of them into every area of their lives.

I adapted this last point from Zig Ziglar's *How to Raise Positive Kids in a Negative World* [3], one of the best books I've read on this subject.

To understand the importance of monitoring the outside stimuli and influences that knock on the doors of your kids' minds, you will need to answer the following question. Suppose I were to gather all of your youth in one auditorium and then stand up before them and say, "Young adults, I'm here to tell you that getting drunk is awesome. Drugs are awesome. You're a nobody if you don't do drugs. To be popular, you need to try some crack cocaine.

"And you need to have all the sex you can; orgies are the best. And get into bestiality and the worship of idols. Murder is definitely something you have to try. And hate your parents. Don't listen to them—they're fools. Now go out and do all of these things. These are great, amazing experiences—please try them." (And then imagine that I added a little rhythm and used some poetic four-letter words.)

More than ninety-nine percent of parents, including those who aren't Christians, would be in an uproar. The news media would be all over it, and everyone would want me dead. I guarantee I would no longer be allowed to speak to or further "motivate" your children. You would be so mad and upset.

Yet so many parents, including Christians, have no problem at all with what their kids listen to as far as music is concerned. Most parents would be shocked to find out that everything I just said about drugs, sex and murder is being said to their kids every day, all day long, through music. Most parents have no clue to what is going into their kids' minds. Then they are genuinely confused by what is coming out of their kids—their kids' words and their behavior. The parents don't understand the rebellion, hate and anger that exist in their own home.

Understand, I am not saying young people shouldn't be allowed to listen to anything but Christian music because there is a lot of good music out there. But I am saying that there is some heavy, hard stuff out there that your kids should not be allowed to listen to. And you can recognize most of it by just looking at the album covers. For example, if you pick up a CD and on the cover are three girls with everything "popping out" all over the place, you can know that these are probably not the people you want speaking into your daughter's life.

Studies have been conducted that show that kids who listen to heavy rock-and-roll music that has bestiality and other illicitness in it are 1,000 percent more likely to rebel against their parents, use drugs, and even commit suicide.

"Well, they're sixteen years old, and I can't control what they listen to." Yes, you can. You are in charge of their moral conscience until they can make the right choice.

In my own life, I was not able to pick out my own music until my parents felt like I could pick out the right music. That's just how it worked. So it was not until tenth grade that my parents finally said, "We now believe that you can take on the responsibility of choosing the right music. But if you go to the wrong music, we'll take that responsibility away."

I said in a previous chapter that your kids shouldn't get to choose until they choose right. In other words, just because your daughter is sixteen doesn't mean she's ready to choose the right music; she may not be mature enough to handle it.

I challenge you to tell your kids, "Dad's going to take your CD to work today and listen to it. I'm going to get hip today. I'm going to listen to it, and I'm going to find out what's going on in your head because it is very important to me. I will make sure I guard your emotions until you learn to guard them yourself."

I've talked to so many parents who felt like they were doing a good job parenting but were confused because their house was full of rebellion. Their kids were angry and depressed. They hadn't monitored what was going into them—that stimuli from without that has the potential to destroy their kids' lives.

I talked a lot about watching the type of music your kids listen to but, really, the same goes for TV. What are you allowing to come into your living room and into your family's lives?

> You are in charge of their moral conscience until they can make the right choice.

My wife has been talking to me for a while about our kids watching too much television. Just recently, it finally sinks into my little heart, and, suddenly, I'm saying, "My kids are watching too much TV."

Holly says, "I've been saying that for years!"

I answer, "Well, praise God, He finally got through to me."

I encourage you to keep track of just how much TV is going into your kids this week. You will be very surprised, like I was, to find that they could be watching five or more hours a day. And all the while they're watching TV, they're not using their imagination, building their problem-solving skills, strengthening their IQ, developing their relationship skills or getting the physical exercise they need to live healthy, balanced lives in every area. They're just sitting, zoned out, with no memories being built inside them.

As a dad, you are responsible for setting the mood of the home, for guarding the emotions of the home, and for always pointing the home to the love, joy, peace, and happiness. When these characteristics are in your heart as a father, you can effectively guide your children into bright and beautiful futures with happy memories of home and an ongoing relationship with Dad that they will carry into the lives of their own children.

As we finish this journey of ours, I encourage you to go back and reread this book. Statistically, you only remember about twenty percent of what you read the first time. Having read this manuscript many times as the author, I have found myself growing and changing a little bit each time I read it. As I read about the importance of communication, for example, I think, I have forgotten lately to be sensitive to my family's needs in that area. Then I'll think, I need to reevaluate my values and priorities. I need to spend some more quality time with my wife. I need to plan for more family time, creating lifetime memories.

I also remember, I need to be sensitive to my children's secret place, their inner world, as they share places in their heart with me that are vulnerable and sacred. I don't want to miss that "window."

As I read further along, I allow it to sink deep into my heart and mind, I need to continually see myself as the coach of our team. I need to plan some more Bible time with the kids. I need to continue to set the right mood in my home. My wife would laugh, because often when she entered my office, my eyes would be welled up with tears, and I'd say, "Boy, this is good. It just changed my life."

So as strange as it sounds, each time I read this book, it helps me grow and keep changing. It helps me

get back on-track as I fulfill my vision for great fathering. Every one of us gets busy in life with things we need
to do. If we don't remind ourselves of the things that are
important, we can slip into neglecting the things that really matter in life.

I challenge you to never stop growing and changing. Get that vision inside you, in your heart and mind,
for developing a great relationship with your children.
Then keep that vision going so that at the end of your life,
your children will be able to say about you, "There lies
my best friend, my hero, my dad."

[3]Ziglar, Zig, *How to Raise Positive Kids in a Negative World*. New
York : Ballantine Books, a division of Random House, Inc., 1989.

Featured Products by Winword Authors:

Scot Anderson
Dr. C. Thomas Anderson
Maureen Anderson
Jason Anderson

Think Like a Billionaire, Become a Billionaire

Who's the Boss?

What in Health do You Want?

Finding Solitude With God

Wisdom Wins 1

Wisdom Wins 2

Confessing God's Word

Damaged DNA

Me, My Country, My God

To order or for more information,
visit Winword Publishing House online at:

www.winwordpublishing.com

Or contact us at:
480-985-6156
or
www.DadMomBook.com

Winword
publishing house